Step-by-Step
Baking

igloobooks
.com

Published in 2012
by Igloo Books Ltd
Cottage Farm
Sywell
Northants
NN6 0BJ
www.igloobooks.com

Food photography and recipe development: PhotoCuisine UK
Front and back cover images © PhotoCuisine UK

HUN001 0812
2 4 6 8 10 9 7 5 3 1
ISBN: 978-0-85780-734-2

Printed and manufactured in China

Step-by-Step
Baking

Contents

6. Blueberry Muffins

8. Stewed Apple Muffins

10. Lemon Muffins

12. Raisin Cookies

14. Chocolate and Pecan Muffins

16. Honey Scones

18. Petit Fours

20. Coconut Cookies

22. Almond Cookies

24. Poppy Seed Palmiers

26. Chocolate Chip Cookies

28. Chocolate Cookies

30. Shortbread

32. Hazelnut Brownies

35. Mini Ginger Cakes

38. Oatmeal Cookies

40. King's Cakes

42. Rolled Biscuits

44. Violet and Orange Soufflé

47. Scones

50. Sweet Macaroons

52. Thyme Macaroons

54. Amaretti

56. Apple Toffee Muffins

58. Viennese Whirls

60. Pistachio Brownies

62. Chocolate Shortbread

64. Herb Cakes

66. Blackberry and Raspberry Cakes

68 Granary Bread

70. Tomato Bread

72. Sweetcorn Bread

74. Small Breads

76. Walnut and Cheese Loaf

78. Spinach Savoury Cakes

80. Cheese Sticks

82. Poppy Seed Loaf

84. Small Bread Loaves

86. Gouda Loaf

88. Rosemark Focaccia

90. Olive Bread Sticks

92. Walnut Bread

94. Parmesan and Basil Rolls

96. Courgette and Rosemary Rocaccias

98. Cheese Loaf

100. Cheese Scones

102. Sesame Seed Rolls

104. Mocha Cake

107. Chocolate Pudding

110. Chocolate Fudge Cake

112. Billberry Pie

114. Chocolate and Walnut Sponge

116. Carrot and Cinnamon Cake

118. Pineapple Coconut Tart

120. Italian Rice Tart

122. Chocolate, Almond and Toffee Cake

124. Breton Cake

126. Poppy Seed Cake

128. Pear Upside-down Cake

130. Sponge Cake

132. Lemon Cake

135. Sticky Toffee Pudding

138. Frambosier

140. Fudge Tart

142. Pound Cake

144. Cheese Soufflé

147. Lemon Meringue Pie

150. Apple Pie

152. Orange Cake

154. Marble Cake

156. Chocolate Cake

158. Chocolate Log Cake

161. Blueberry Pies

164. Orange and Marmalade Kumquat

166. Fig Cake

168. Plum Cake

170. Cherry Pies

172. Brownie Yoghurts

175. Chocolate and Almond Moelleux

178. Corn Cake

180. Summer Fruits Tart

182. Yoghurt and Fruit Cake

184. Strawberry Paris Brest

187. Sugar Bun

190. Index

Blueberry Muffins

Ingredients

450 g / 1 lb / 3 cups plain (all-purpose) flour, sifted

225 g / 8 oz / 1 cup caster (superfine) sugar

125 ml / 4 ½ fl. oz / ½ cup plain yoghurt

75 g / 3 oz / ¾ stick butter, melted and cooled

2 medium eggs

250 g / 9 oz / 1 ⅔ cups blueberries

1 tsp vanilla extract

1 tsp baking powder

pinch of salt

SERVES 18 | PREP TIME 15 minutes | COOKING TIME 25-30 minutes

Prepare and measure all of the ingredients. Preheat the oven to 180°C (160°C fan) / 350F / gas 4. Line 2 cupcake trays with 18 cupcake cases.

Combine the flour, sugar, salt and baking powder in a large mixing bowl.

In a separate bowl, whisk together the butter, yoghurt, eggs and vanilla extract until smooth. Pour into the dry ingredients and mix together until just incorporated.

Fold in the blueberries at this point until evenly distributed.

Spoon into the cupcake cases and bake for 15-18 minutes until risen, golden and springy to the touch. Remove and transfer the muffins to wire racks to cool. Once cool, stack the muffins in pairs and tie together using string.

Stewed Apple Muffins

Ingredients

450 g / 1 lb / 2 cups Bramley apples, peeled
and cored

85 g / 3 ½ oz / ½ cup dark brown sugar

450 g / 1 lb / 3 cups self-raising flour, sifted

85 g / 3 ½ oz / ½ cup dark muscovado sugar

110 ml / 4 fl. oz / ½ cup sunflower oil

125 ml / 4 ½ fl. oz / ½ cup whole milk

1 tsp baking powder

2 large eggs

½ tsp vanilla extract

pinch of salt

MAKES 12 | PREP TIME 15-20 minutes | COOKING TIME 40-45 minutes

Measure and prepare all of the ingredients. Preheat the oven to 180°C
(160° fan) / 375F / gas 4.

Line a 12-hole muffin tin with the muffin paper cases.

Place the cooking apple and dark brown sugar in a saucepan with a sprinkling of cold water.

Heat over a medium heat stirring occasionally, until softened, then remove from the heat and mash until smooth.

Combine the flour, baking powder, dark muscovado sugar and sunflower oil together in a large mixing bowl and mix well until smooth. Fold the apple mixture into the muffin batter and stir well to incorporate.

Spoon into the cases and bake for 20-25 minutes until golden and risen. Remove from the oven and transfer to a wire rack to cool. Remove the cases from the muffins before serving warm or cold.

Lemon Muffins

Ingredients

225 g / 8 oz / 1 ½ cups self-raising flour

1 tsp baking powder (soda)

110 g / 4 oz / ½ cup caster (superfine) sugar

110 ml / 4 fl. oz / ½ cup sunflower oil

75 ml / 3 fl. oz / ⅓ cup whole milk

1 large egg, beaten

1 lemon, juiced and zested

½ tsp lemon extract

a pinch of salt

To garnish

225 g / 8 oz / 2 sticks unsalted butter, softened

250 g / 9 oz / 2 cups icing (confectioner's) sugar

55 g / 2 oz / ¼ cup cream cheese

1 lemon, juiced

2 tbsp candied lemon peel

MAKES 12 | PREP TIME 10-15 minutes | COOKING TIME 30-40 minutes

Preheat the oven to 170°C (150°C fan) / 325F / gas 3. Line a 12 hole muffin tin with muffin cases.

Sift together the flour, baking powder and salt into a large mixing bowl. Add the sugar and stir until combined.

3

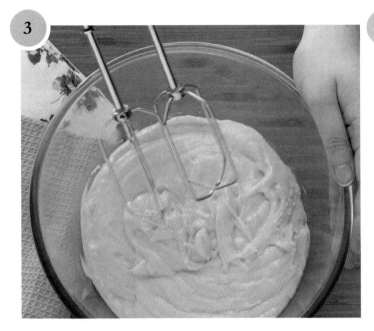

Add the egg, sunflower oil, milk, lemon juice, zest and the lemon extract and bring together with a whisk until you have a lightly mixed batter.

4

Spoon into the cases and bake for 18-22 minutes until risen and springy to the touch. Remove and allow to cool for a few minutes before turning out onto a wire rack to cool completely.

5

Prepare the icing by beating together the icing sugar, butter, cream cheese and lemon juice with an electric whisk until you have a smooth icing.

6

Remove the muffins from their cases and top with large tablespoons of the icing. Garnish with a strip of candied lemon zest before serving.

Raisin Cookies

Ingredients

500 g / 1 lb 2 oz / 3 ⅓ cups plain (all-purpose) flour

225 g / 8 oz / 2 sticks unsalted butter, softened

110 g / 4 oz / ½ cup caster (superfine) sugar

110 g / 4 oz / ⅔ cup light brown sugar

100 g / 3 ½ oz / ½ cup raisins

2 small eggs

1 tsp ground clove

½ tsp ground all-spice

pinch of salt

MAKES 24 | PREP TIME 10 minutes | COOKING TIME 25-30 minutes

Prepare and measure all of the ingredients. Preheat the oven to 180°C (160°C fan) / 350F / gas 4.

Cream together the butter, ground clove, all-spice and sugars together in a bowl until smooth for about 2 minutes.

Beat in one egg at a time, mixing well between additions. Beat in the flour in thirds with a pinch of salt, taking care not to overwork the dough.

Add the raisins and stir them in well.

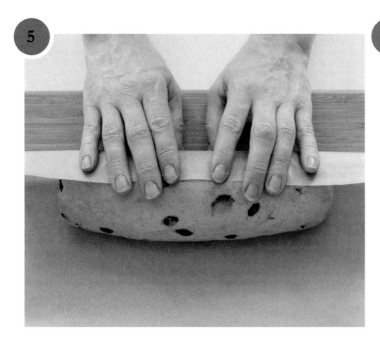

Roll into a Swiss roll shape (about 5-6cm in diameter) and wrap in parchment paper. Chill until firm; roughly 1 hour.

When ready, slice discs of dough roughly 1 cm thick. Arrange on greased and lined trays, spaced apart. Bake for 15-20 minutes until golden brown. Remove and allow to cool before moving to a wire rack to cool completely.

Chocolate and Pecan Muffins

Ingredients

250 g / 9 oz / 2 ¼ sticks unsalted butter, softened

a little extra butter, for greasing

175 g / 6 oz / ¾ cup caster (superfine) sugar

250 g / 9 oz / 1 ⅔ cups bread flour

110 g / 4 oz / ⅔ cup good-quality dark chocolate, finely chopped

150 g / 5 oz / 1 cup cocoa powder

85 g / 3 oz / ⅓ cup pecans, finely chopped

4 large eggs

85 ml / 3 fl. oz / ⅓ cup whole milk

1 tbsp baking powder (soda)

a pinch of salt

MAKES 12 | PREP TIME 10-15 minutes | COOKING TIME 20 minutes

Preheat the oven to 200°C (180° fan) / 400F / gas 6. Measure and prepare the ingredients.

Grease and line the insides of 12 ramekin moulds with a little butter and small sheets of greaseproof paper.

3

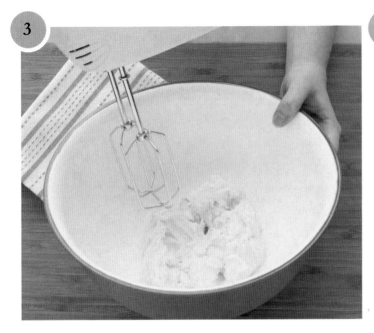

Cream together the butter and sugar in a bowl, until pale and fluffy. Add the eggs, one at a time, beating well between additions. After the last egg has been added, continue beating the mixture for 4-5 minutes.

4

Sift in the flour, baking powder, cocoa powder and a pinch of salt and fold gently into the mixture. Add the milk and fold to loosen the mixture a little.

5

Fold in the chopped chocolate and most of the pecans, reserving 1 tbsp to garnish the muffins before serving.

6

Spoon the mixture into the ramekins and arrange on baking trays. Bake for 20 minutes. Remove from the oven and cool on top of a wire rack. Garnish with the pecans before serving.

Honey Scones

Ingredients

225 g / 8 oz / 1 ½ cups plain (all-purpose)
flour, sifted

a little plain (all-purpose) flour, for dusting

55 g / 2 oz / ½ stick butter, cubed

55 ml / 2 fl. oz / ¼ cup honey

30 g / 1 oz / 2 tbsp caster (suoerfine) sugar

110 ml / 4 fl. oz / ½ cup whole milk

1 tsp cream of tartar

1 tsp bicarbonate (baking) of soda

1 small egg, beaten

55 g / 2 oz / ¼ cup sesame seeds

SERVES 12 | PREP TIME 10 minutes | COOKING TIME 25-30 minutes

Preheat the oven to 190°C (170°C fan) / 375F / gas 5. Grease and line 2 baking trays with greaseproof paper. Sift together the flour, cream of tartar and bicarbonate of soda into a large mixing bowl. Rub the cubed butter into the flour until it resembles breadcrumbs.

Stir through the honey and sugar, then add the milk and stir until you have a rough dough.

3

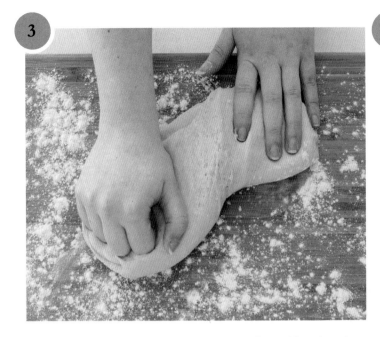

Turn the dough out onto a lightly floured work surface and knead gently for a few minutes until more even.

4

Roll the dough into a round roughly 2 cm thick. Punch out rounds of dough using a 6-7 cm cookie cutter.

5

Gather up the remaining dough and re-roll to 2 cm thickness before punching out more rounds of dough. Arrange on the baking trays and brush their tops lightly with the beaten egg.

6

Sprinkle a teaspoon of sesame seeds on top of each and bake for 15-20 minutes until golden and risen. Remove from the oven and transfer to a wire rack to cool before serving.

Petit Fours

Ingredients

110 g / 4 oz / ⅔ cup self-raising flour, sifted

55 g / 2 oz / ½ cup ground almonds

110 g / 4 oz / ½ cup caster (superfine) sugar

110 g / 4 oz / ½ cup margarine

30 ml / 1 fl. oz / 2 tbsp whole milk

2 medium eggs

½ tsp almond extract

24 blanched almonds

MAKES 24 | PREP TIME 10 minutes | COOKING TIME 20-25 minutes

Measure and prepare all of the ingredients. Preheat the oven to 180°C (160° fan) / 350F / gas 4. Line 2 mini cupcake trays with cupcake cases.

Combine all the ingredients apart from the blanched almonds in a large mixing bowl and beat using an electric mixer until smooth, scraping down the sides from time to time.

Spoon tablespoons of the mixture into the cupcake cases.

Stud each with a blanched almond. Bake for 10-12 minutes until risen and springy to the touch.

Remove from the oven and let them cool for 5 minutes before removing to a wire rack to finish cooling. Serve warm or cold.

Coconut Cookies

Ingredients

200 g / 7 oz / 1 ⅓ cups plain (all-purpose)
flour, sifted

a little extra plain flour, for dusting

150 g / 5 oz / ⅔ cup margarine, softened

75 g / 3 oz / ⅓ cup caster (superfine) sugar

110 g / 4 oz / 1 cup desiccated coconut

½ tsp bicarbonate of (baking) soda

½ tsp vanilla extract

a pinch of salt

SERVES 24 | PREP TIME 10 minutes | COOKING TIME 25-30 minutes

1

Prepare and measure all of the ingredients. Preheat the oven to 180°C
(160° fan) / 350F / gas 4.

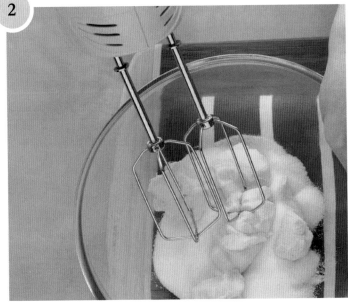

2

In a mixing bowl, cream the margarine and sugar until pale and fluffy
using a handheld electric whisk.

Beat in the flour, bicarbonate of soda and vanilla extract then add the desiccated coconut and knead this dough lightly for 5 minutes.

Roll the dough out on a lightly floured surface to 1cm thickness and cut rounds out of the dough using a 4-5 cm round straight-sided cookie cutter.

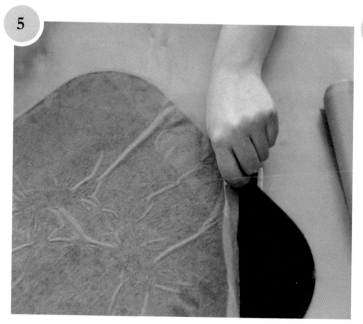

Grease and line a couple of baking trays with greaseproof paper.

Carefully lift onto the baking trays and space them apart. Bake for 12 minutes. Remove from the oven and cool for a few minutes before moving to a wire rack to cool further.

Almond Cookies

Ingredients

240 g / 8 oz / 1 ½ cups plain (all-purpose) flour, sifted

30 g / 1 oz / ¼ cup ground almonds

a little extra plain flour, for dusting

175 g / 6 oz / ¾ cup margarine, softened

75 g / 3 oz / ⅓ cup caster (superfine) sugar

150 g / 5 oz / ⅔ cup blanched almonds

½ tsp vanilla extract

½ tsp bicarbonate (baking) of soda

a pinch of salt

SERVES 24 | PREP TIME 10 minutes | COOKING TIME 25-30 minutes

Prepare and measure all of the ingredients. Preheat the oven to 170°C (150° fan) / 325F / gas 3. Grease and line a couple of baking trays with greaseproof paper.

Cream together the margarine and sugar in a large mixing bowl until pale and fluffy using a handheld electric whisk.

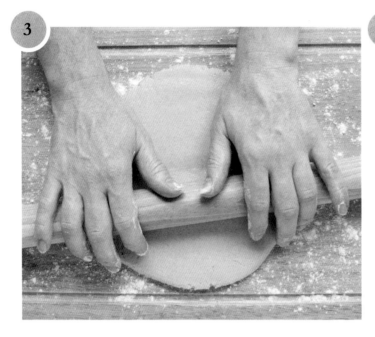

Beat in the flour, bicarbonate of soda and vanilla extract and knead this dough lightly for 5 minutes. Roll the dough out on a lightly floured surface to 1cm thickness.

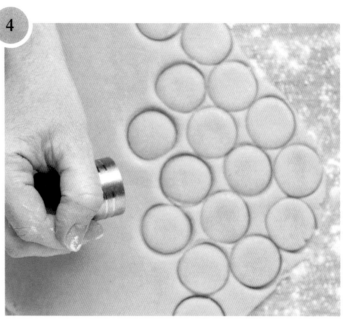

Cut rounds out of the dough using a 3-4 cm straight-sided cookie cutter.

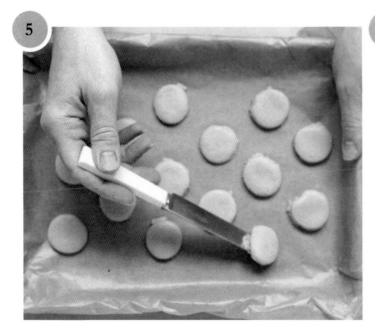

Carefully lift onto the baking trays and space them apart.

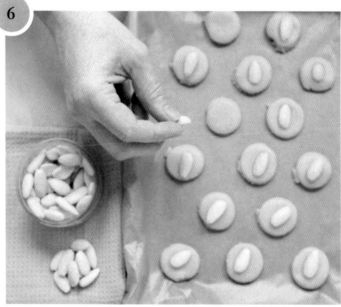

Stud each cookie with a few almonds. Bake for 12 minutes. Remove from the oven and let them cool on the baking tray for a few minutes before moving to a wire rack to cool completely.

Poppy Seed Palmiers

Ingredients

160 g / 5 ½ oz / 1 sheet ready-made puff pastry

a little plain (all-purpose) flour, for dusting

55 g / 2 oz / ¼ cup honey, warmed

30 g / 1 oz / 2 tbsp poppy seeds

SERVES 24 | PREP TIME 10 minutes | COOKING TIME 20-25 minutes

Prepare and measure all of the ingredients. Preheat the oven to 200°C (180° fan) / 400F / gas 6. Grease and line a large baking tray with greaseproof paper.

Roll the puff pastry out on a lightly floured surface into a 10" x 12" rectangle.

3

Brush the surface with the honey, then sprinkle the poppy seeds all over so that they stick to the honey.

4

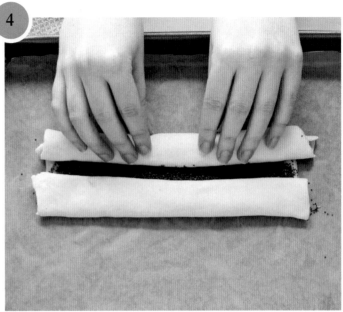

Roll the left hand side of the puff pastry so that it meets the centre of the pastry. Do the same with the right hand side so that it meets the rolled left hand side in the middle. Transfer to the lined baking tray and chill for 45 minutes.

5

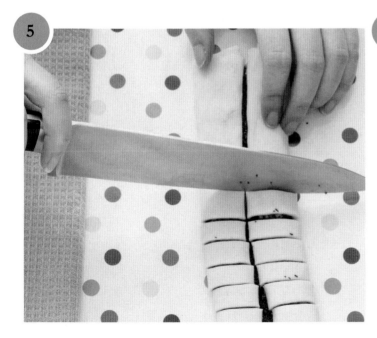

Remove after chilling and cut slices across the rolled pastry roughly 1 cm thick. Pinch the sides of the pastry so that they form a classic Palmier shape. Line a couple of baking trays with greaseproof paper.

6

Transfer the uncooked biscuits to the trays and space them well apart. Bake for 12-15 minutes until golden. Remove from the oven and let them cool for 5 minutes on the trays before removing to a wire rack to finish cooling.

Chocolate Chip Cookies

Ingredients

225 g / 8 oz / 1 ½ cups plain (all-purpose) flour, sifted

110 g / 4 oz / 1 stick unsalted butter, softened

55 g / 2 oz / ⅓ cup light soft brown sugar

55 g / 2 oz / ¼ cup caster (superfine) sugar

½ tsp baking powder

½ tsp bicarbonate (baking) of soda

½ tsp salt

1 large egg, lightly beaten

150 g / 5 oz / 1 cup milk chocolate chips

SERVES 12-14 | PREP TIME 10 minutes | COOKING TIME 20-25 minutes

Prepare and measure the ingredients. Preheat the oven to 180°C (160° fan) / 350F / gas 4. Grease and line a couple of baking trays with greaseproof paper.

In a large bowl, combine the flour, chocolate chips, baking powder, bicarbonate of soda and salt.

3

4

In a separate bowl, beat together the butter and sugars using an electric whisk until light and fluffy. Gradually add the beaten egg by the tablespoon whilst whisking simultaneously. Fold in the flour mixture until incorporated.

Take large tablespoons of the mixture and roll into balls. Line and grease two trays and arrange the balls of dough, spaced well apart.

5

Flatten each ball using a flat palm. Bake for 10 minutes. Remove from the oven and allow to cool for 5 minutes before removing to a wire rack to finish cooling. Serve stacked on plates.

Chocolate Cookies

Ingredients

110 g / 4 oz / ⅔ cup plain (all-purpose) flour, sifted

75 g / 3 oz / ¾ stick unsalted butter, chilled and cubed

55 g / 2 oz / ⅓ cup icing (confectioner's) sugar

55 g / 2 oz / ½ cup good-quality cocoa powder, sifted

110 g / 4 oz / ⅔ cup dark chocolate chips

1 large egg

½ tsp vanilla extract

½ tsp salt

MAKES 12 | PREP TIME 10 minutes | COOKING TIME 25-30 minutes

Measure and prepare all of the ingredients. Combine together the icing sugar, cocoa powder, flour and salt in a large mixing bowl.

Rub the butter into this mixture until it resembles fine breadcrumbs.

Add the egg, dark chocolate chips and vanilla extract and mix until a stiff dough forms.

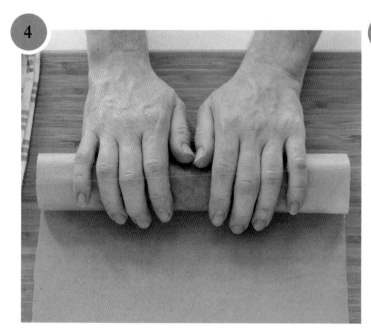

Gather up and roll into a sausage shape with a diameter of 8-10 cm. Wrap in greaseproof paper and chill in the fridge for at least 30 minutes.

Grease and line 2 trays with greaseproof paper. Preheat the oven to 180°C (160°C) / 350F / gas 4. Use a cutter to cut out 1 cm thick cookies from the dough. Arrange on the trays and bake for 12-14 minutes. Remove and allow to cool for 10 minutes before transferring to a wire rack to cool further.

Shortbread

Ingredients

200 g / 7 oz / 1 ⅓ cups plain (all-purpose) flour, sifted

a little extra plain flour, for dusting

150 g / 5 oz / ⅔ cup margarine, softened

75 g / 3 oz / ⅓ cup caster (superfine) sugar

½ tsp vanilla extract

½ tsp bicarbonate (baking) of soda

a pinch of salt

300 ml / 10 ½ fl. oz / 1 ⅓ cup double cream

2 tbsp icing (confectioner's) sugar

To garnish

450 g / 1 lb / 3 cups raspberries

2 tbsp icing (confectioner's) sugar

5-6 small sprigs of mint

SERVES 8 | PREP TIME 10-15 minutes | COOKING TIME 40-45 minutes

Prepare and measure all of the ingredients. Preheat the oven to 150°C (130°C fan) / 300F / gas 2. Grease and line a couple of baking trays with greaseproof paper.

Cream together the margarine and sugar in a large mixing bowl until pale and fluffy using a handheld electric whisk.

Beat in the flour, bicarbonate of soda and vanilla extract and knead this dough lightly for 5 minutes.

Roll the dough out on a lightly floured surface to 1cm thickness and cut rounds out of the dough using a 7-8 cm fluted cookie cutter. Carefully lift onto the baking trays and space them apart.

Bake for 12-15 minutes until set but uncoloured. Remove from the oven and let them cool on the baking tray for a few minutes before moving to a wire rack to cool completely.

As the cookies are cooling, whip together the double cream with 2 tbsp of icing sugar in a bowl until it forms soft peaks. Spoon 2 tbsp of the cream on top of the cookies. Dot with raspberries on top of each cookie and garnish with a sprig of mint leaves. Dust lightly with the remaining icing sugar just before serving.

Hazelnut Brownies

Ingredients

350 g / 12 oz / 2 ⅓ cups dark chocolate,
chopped

225 g / 8 oz / 2 sticks unsalted butter

250 g / 9 oz / 1 ⅓ cups light soft brown sugar

110 g / 4 oz / ¾ cup plain (all-purpose) flour

150 g / 5 oz / 1 cup hazelnuts (cob nuts),
roughly chopped

3 large eggs

1 tsp baking powder

a pinch of salt

SERVES 8 | PREP TIME 15 minutes | COOKING TIME 45 minutes

Preheat the oven to 170°C (150°C fan) /325F / gas 3. Prepare and measure all of the ingredients and break up the chocolate. Grease and line the base of a 5" square baking.

Melt the chocolate and butter together in a saucepan over a medium-low heat, stirring occasionally until they are smooth. Remove from the heat and allow to cool a little.

In a bowl, whisk the eggs until they are thick then add the sugar and continue to whisk until glossy.

Beat in the melted chocolate mixture, and then fold in the flour and baking powder until incorporated.

Pour into the baking tray and tap lightly a few times to release any trapped air bubbles.

6

Scatter the chopped hazelnuts on top, reserving 2 tbsp for garnishing. Bake for 45 minutes. Remove from the oven and set the tray on top of a wire rack, letting it cool for 45 minutes.

7

Once cool enough, turn out of the tin and carefully move onto a chopping board. Cut the block of brownie into squares and arrange them stacked on sheets of greaseproof paper, garnished with the remaining hazelnuts.

Mini Ginger Cakes

Ingredients

110 g / 4 oz / ½ cup caster (superfine) sugar

110 g / 4 oz / ⅔ cup self-raising flour, sifted

110 g / 4 oz / 1 stick butter, softened

2 tbsp cornflour, sifted

2 medium eggs

2" fresh ginger, peeled and finely grated

2 tbsp syrup from crystallized ginger jar

a pinch of salt

MAKES 12 | PREP TIME 10 minutes | COOKING TIME 20-25 minutes

Prepare and measure all of the ingredients. Preheat the oven to 180°C (160° fan) / 350F / gas 4. Spray the inside of a fluted 12 hole cupcake tin with cooking spray.

Combine the sugar, flour, butter, syrup and eggs in a large mixing bowl.

3

Beat using an electric mixer for 2 minutes until smooth, scraping down the sides from time to time.

4

Add a pinch of salt, grated ginger and cornflour and blend well.

5

Spoon the batter into the cupcake tin and bake for 12-16 minutes until golden, risen and slightly springy to the touch.

6

Remove from the oven and let the cakes cool in the tin for 10 minutes.

7

Turning out and stack on a serving platter. Serve warm or cold.

Oatmeal Cookies

Ingredients

175 g / 6 oz / 1 ½ sticks unsalted butter, softened

175 g / 6 oz / 1 cup soft brown sugar

1 large egg

1 tbsp honey

225 g / 8 oz / 1 ½ cups plain (all-purpose) flour, sifted

350 g / 12 oz / 3 cups rolled oats

1 tsp vanilla extract

½ tsp ground cinnamon

½ tsp salt

MAKES 18 | PREP TIME 15 minutes | COOKING TIME 30 minutes

Preheat the oven to 180°C (160° fan) / 350F / gas 4. Grease and line 2 baking sheets. Prepare and measure all of the ingredients.

In a bowl, cream together the butter and sugar until pale and fluffy.

Add the honey, egg and vanilla extract and beat well again.

In a separate mixing bowl, sift together the flour, salt and bicarbonate of soda. Beat into the creamed butter and sugar mixture until you have a cookie dough.

Fold in the rolled oats until incorporated. Take large tablespoon of the dough and roll between lightly oiled palms.

Place on the baking sheets, spaced apart and flatten with a straight palm. Bake for 18 minutes. Remove from the oven and to cool on the baking sheets before moving to a wire rack to finish cooling.

King's Cakes

Ingredients

320 g / 11 oz / 2 sheets ready-made puff pastry

plain (all-purpose) flour, for dusting

110 g / 4 oz / 1/2 cup caster (superfine) sugar

110 g / 4 oz / 1 stick unsalted butter, softened

110 g / 4 oz / 1 cup ground almonds

1 tbsp Cognac

1 medium egg, beaten

1 medium egg yolk, beaten

2 tbsp apricot jam

To garnish

1 tbsp sugar nibs

MAKES 4 | PREP TIME 10 minutes | COOKING TIME 30-35 minutes

Preheat the oven to 200°C (180° fan) / 400F / gas 6. Prepare and measure all of the ingredients.

Roll each sheet of puff pastry out on a lightly floured work surface. Use a fluted cookie cutter to stamp out 4 rounds from each sheet of puff pastry so that you have 8 rounds in total.

Slide 4 of the rounds onto a sheet of greaseproof paper and place on top of a baking tray. Spread the apricot jam on top of the rounds to within 1 cm of their edges.

Combine the butter and sugar in a food processor and blitz until smooth. Add the egg and pulse until incorporated. Spoon the mixture into a mixing bowl and fold through the ground almonds and the Cognac.

Spread the mixture on top of the jam, then wet the rims of the pastry with a little water. Cover with the remaining rounds of pastry, sealing the edges well.

Mark the tops with a sharp knife in the pattern of curved spokes. Brush with the beaten egg yolk and bake for 20 minutes. Remove from the oven and let them cool on wire racks. Garnish with sugar nibs.

Rolled Biscuits

Ingredients

110 g / 4 oz / ½ cup caster (superfine) sugar

110 g / 4 oz / ⅔ cup plain (all-purpose) flour, sifted

55 g / 2 oz / ½ stick unsalted butter, softened

½ tsp vanilla extract

4 medium egg whites

a pinch of salt

MAKES 12-14 | PREP TIME 5-10 minutes | COOKING TIME 15-20 minutes

Preheat the oven to 180°C (160°C fan) / 350F / gas 4. Measure and prepare all of the ingredients.

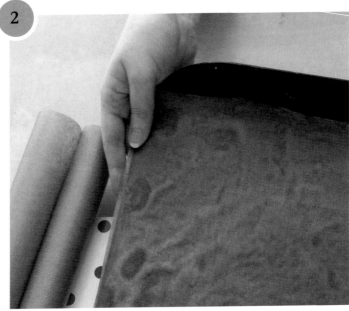

Grease and line a couple of large baking tray with parchment paper.

3

Beat together the butter, vanilla extract and sugar in a mixing bowl until pale and fluffy.

4

Beat in the egg whites until incorporated, then sift in the flour and beat again until smooth.

5

Spoon tablespoons of the mixture onto the baking tray and use the back of the spoon to spread into circle shapes 10-12 cm in diameter. Bake for 6-8 minutes until the edges are just starting to colour.

6

Remove from the oven and carefully slide each one onto a sharpening steel and roll. Slide them off the steel and place on a wire rack. If they cool too much before you shape them, return the tray to the oven for a minute until they become soft enough to mould.

Violet and Orange Soufflé

Ingredients

30 g / 1 oz / ¼ stick unsalted butter,
for greasing
110 g / 4 oz / ½ cup golden caster (superfine)
sugar
4 medium egg whites
2 medium egg yolks
2 small oranges, juiced and zested
3 tsp cornflour
1 tbsp plain (all-purpose) flour

110 ml / 4 fl. oz / ½ cup whole milk
110 ml / 4 fl. oz / ½ cup double cream
a pinch of salt

To garnish
4 tsp candied violets
1 large orange
110 g / 4 oz / ½ cup caster (superfine) sugar
225 ml / 8 fl. oz / 1 cup water

SERVES 4 | PREP TIME 15 minutes | COOKING TIME 45-55 minutes

Prepare and measure all of the ingredients. Brush 4 ceramic wide-rimmed ramekins with the butter. Add 1 tsp of the sugar to each ramekin and coat the insides turning well. Chill the ramekins until needed.

Remove the peel from the orange. Use a sharp knife to remove the white pith from the back of the zest pieces. Julienne the zest and place in a saucepan of cold water. Bring to the boil then drain.

3

Combine 225 ml of water with 110 g of caster sugar in a saucepan. Bring to a simmer until you have a clear syrup. Add the zest and simmer for 5 minutes. Remove and leave to cool and dry.

4

Whisk together the cream, cornflour and flour. Heat the milk until it comes to the boil. Remove from the heat and whisk into the cream mixture. Transfer back to the saucepan and heat, whisking until thickened. Remove and stir in the orange juice and zest.

5

Whisk together the yolks and sugar. Add the hot milk and cream, whisk and transfer to the saucepan. Cook, stirring continuously, until thickened. Remove and spoon into a bowl and leave to cool.

6

Beat the egg whites with a pinch of salt to soft peaks in a separate, clean mixing bowl. Pre-heat the oven to 180°C (160° fan) / 350F / gas 4. Once the custard mixture has cooled, fold the egg whites into it, working quickly.

7

Spoon into the ramekins. Place on a baking tray and bake for 15 minutes until the soufflés rise. Remove from the oven and garnish with 1 tsp of candied violets and a few strips of candied orange zest before serving.

Scones

Ingredients

200 g / 7 oz / 1 ⅓ cups plain flour

100 g / 4 oz / ½ cup raisins

50 g / 2 oz / ¼ cup caster (superfine) sugar

50 g / 2 oz / ½ stick butter, softened

75 ml / 3 fl. oz / ⅓ cup milk

½ tsp baking powder (soda)

¼ tsp salt

SERVES 6 | PREP TIME 15 minutes | COOKING TIME 12 minutes

Preheat the oven to 200°C (180° fan) / 400F / gas 6. Prepare and measure all of the ingredients.

Mix the flour, baking powder, sugar and salt.

3

Add the butter cut into pieces.

4

Crush using your fingertips until the mix is crumbly.

5

Pour the milk in and the raisins, then mix until the dough is consistent. If it is too dry, add some milk. If too sticky, sprinkle a little flour.

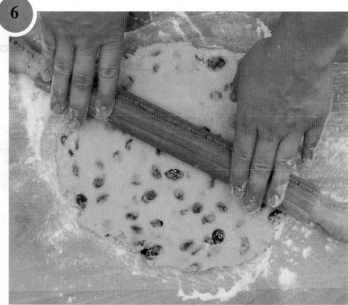

6

Place the dough on a floured surface and roll to a thickness of 1 cm / 0.5 inch.

7

Cut into discs of 5 cm diameter using a cookie cutter.

8

Coat the tops with a little milk and bake for 12 minutes on a sheet of baking paper. Once cooked, remove and leave to cool on a wire rack.

Sweet Macaroons

Ingredients

For the macaroons

125 g / 4 ½ oz / 1 cup icing (confectioner's)
sugar, sifted

75 g / 3 oz / ¾ cup ground almonds

30 g / 1 oz / 2 tbsp cocoa powder, sifted

2 medium egg whites

a pinch of salt

For the filling

110 g / 4 oz / ⅔ cups dark chocolate,
chopped

125 ml / 4 ½ fl. oz / ½ cup double cream

MAKES 32 | PREP TIME 15-20 minutes | COOKING TIME 10 minutes

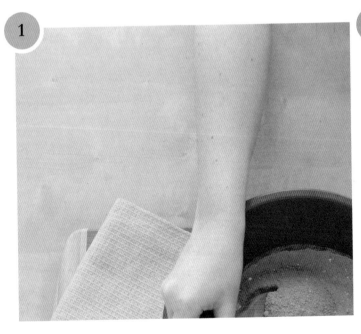

Preheat the oven to 180°C (160° fan) / 350F / gas 4. Grease and line 2
baking trays with greaseproof paper. Combine the ground almonds, cocoa
powder and icing sugar together in a bowl.

Beat the egg whites in a separate bowl with a pinch of salt until stiff
peaks form.

Fold the egg whites into the ground almond mixture until incorporated. Spoon into piping bags fitted with a 3-4 cm in diameter straight-sided piping nozzle.

Pipe 4 cm rounds onto the baking trays, spaced apart. Leave them to set on the trays for 15 minutes, then bake for 10 minutes until just set. Remove from the oven and allow them to cool for 10 minutes.

Place the chocolate in a heatproof bowl. Bring the cream to the boil in a saucepan, then remove from the heat and pour over the chocolate. Stir until the chocolate melts and is smooth.

Let the ganache cool and thicken for 10 minutes, then spread half of the macaroons with 1 tsp of the ganache filling. Sandwich together with the other half of the macaroon discs to complete them.

Thyme Macaroons

Ingredients

110 g / 4 oz / ⅔ cup plain (all-purpose) flour, sifted

extra plain (all-purpose) flour, for dusting

55 g / 2 oz / ½ cup Parmesan, grated

55 g / 2 oz / ½ stick unsalted butter, melted

1 small egg yolk

1 tsp dried thyme

1 tbsp fresh thyme leaves, finely chopped

1 tsp pink peppercorns, finely ground

½ tsp salt

For the filling

225 g / 8 oz / 1 cup cream cheese

110 g / 4 oz / 1 cup Roquefort, crumbled

To garnish

sprigs of thyme

½ tsp pink peppercorns, crushed

MAKES 12-14 | PREP TIME 15 minutes | COOKING TIME 12 minutes

1

Prepare and measure all of the ingredients. Grate the Parmesan cheese and crumble the Roquefort into small pieces.

2

Sieve the flour into a bowl and add the butter, Parmesan, pink peppercorn, dried and fresh thyme and salt. Pulse in a food processor.

Pulse until the mixture resembles fine breadcrumbs. Add the egg yolk and pulse again until the mixture comes together to form a dough.

Turn the mixture out onto a work surface and form into a ball. Wrap in film and chill for 15 minutes. Preheat the oven to 180°C (160° fan) / 350F / gas 4. Grease and line 2 baking trays with greaseproof paper.

Roll out the dough on a floured surface, to 1 cm thick. Use a cookie cutter to punch out rounds of the cookie dough. Lift carefully onto the lined trays and bake for 12 minutes until golden in colour.

Remove from the oven and cool. Beat together the Roquefort and cream cheese. Spoon the filling onto half of the bases of the macaroons. Sandwich together with the remainder and garnish with thyme and pink peppercorns.

Amaretti

Ingredients

350 g / 12 oz / 3 cups ground almonds

350 g / 12 oz / 1 ½ cups caster (superfine)
sugar

4 large egg whites

30 ml / 1 fl. oz / 2 tbsp Amaretto liquor

a pinch of salt

MAKES 24 | PREP TIME 10 minutes | COOKING TIME 20-25 minutes

Measure and prepare all of the ingredients. Preheat the oven to 170°C (150° fan) / 325F / gas 3. Grease and line a couple of baking trays with greaseproof paper.

Whisk the egg whites with a pinch of salt in a large, clean mixing bowl until they form stiff peaks.

Add the sugar and ground almonds and fold in gently until you have an even, smooth paste.

Add the Amaretto liquor and fold through gently using a wooden spoon.

Spoon teaspoons of the mixture onto the baking sheets, making sure they are well spaced apart.

Bake for 12-15 minutes until brown and cracked in appearance. Remove from the oven and let them cool on their trays before serving on plates.

Apple Toffee Muffins

Ingredients

450 g / 1 lb / 2 cups Bramley apples, peeled and cored

75 ml / 3 fl. oz / ⅓ cup dulce de leche

450 g / 1 lb / 3 cups self-raising flour, sifted

75 g / 3 oz / ⅓ cup caster (superfine) sugar

110 ml / 4 fl. oz / ½ cup sunflower oil

225 ml / 8 fl. oz / 1 cup whole milk

2 large eggs

½ tsp vanilla extract

pinch of salt

To garnish

225 ml / 8 fl. oz / 1 cup dulce de leche

a pinch of sea salt

SERVES 12 | PREP TIME 15-20 minutes | COOKING TIME 40-45 minutes

Prepare and measure all of the ingredients. Preheat the oven to 180°C (160° fan) / 375F / gas 4. Spray the insides of 12 individual muffin ramekins with cooking spray.

Place the cooking apple in a saucepan with a sprinkling of cold water. Heat over a medium heat stirring occasionally, until softened, then remove from the heat. Add the dulce de leche and beat well until the mixture is smooth.

Combine the flour, caster sugar and sunflower oil together in a large mixing bowl and mix well until smooth.

Fold the apple mixture into the muffin batter and stir well to incorporate.

Spoon into the muffin cases and bake for 20-25 minutes until golden, risen and a toothpick comes out clean from their centres. Remove from the oven when ready and transfer to a wire rack to cool.

Once cool, prick the tops of the muffins all over with a toothpick. Warm the dulce de leche for the garnish in a small saucepan, stirring a few times until smooth. Add a pinch of sea salt and stir well. Pour the dulce de leche over the muffins, letting it seep into them. Serve warm or cold.

Viennese Whirls

Ingredients

For the biscuits

250 g / 9 oz / 2 ⅙ sticks unsalted butter, softened

75 g / 3 oz / ⅔ cup icing (confectioner's) sugar

225 g / 8 oz / 1 ½ cups plain (all-purpose) flour

75 g / 3 oz / ½ cup cornflour

For the garnish

225 ml / 8 fl. oz / 1 cup double cream

½ tsp vanilla extract

225 g / 8 oz / 1 cup smooth strawberry jam

2 tbsp icing (confectioner's) sugar, for dusting

MAKES 8-10 | PREP TIME 10 minutes | COOKING TIME 35-40 minutes

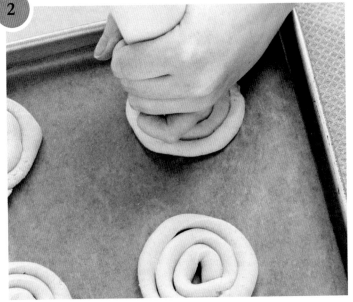

Measure and prepare all of the ingredients. Preheat the oven to 170°C (150° fan) / 325F / gas 3. Grease and line a couple of baking trays with greaseproof paper.

Sift together the flour, icing sugar and cornflour for the biscuits into a bowl. Add the butter and beat everything with a wooden spoon until you have a smooth paste. Spoon into a piping bag with a large straight-sided nozzle. Pipe large rounds of the mixture onto the baking trays.

3

Take a sharp knife and draw lines coming away from the centre of the rounds so that you create a pattern like the spokes of a wheel. Bake for 12-15 minutes until they are a light golden brown in colour.

4

Remove from the oven and leave to cool for a few minutes before moving to a wire rack to finish cooling. Meanwhile, whip together the double cream and vanilla extract in a bowl until soft peaks form. To assemble the biscuits, spread the base of half of the cookies evenly with the jam.

5

Spoon generous teaspoons of the cream on top, then place another cooking on top with the base of sandwiching the cream. Stack the biscuits and dust with icing sugar before serving.

Pistachio Brownies

Ingredients

225 g / 8 oz / 2 sticks unsalted butter, cubed

160 g / 5 ½ oz / 1 cup good-quality dark chocolate, chopped

75 g / 3 oz / ½ cup plain (all-purpose) flour, sifted

55 g / 2 oz / ⅓ cup good-quality cocoa powder, sifted

55 g / 2 oz / ¼ cup caster (superfine) sugar

175 g / 6 oz / 1 cup soft light brown sugar

110 g / 4 oz / 1 cup shelled pistachios, roughly chopped

55 g / 2 oz / ½ cup pecans, roughly chopped

3 large eggs

a few drops of vanilla extract

To garnish

2 tbsp icing (confectioner's) sugar

SERVES 8 | PREP TIME 15 minutes | COOKING TIME 55 minutes

Prepare and measure all of the ingredients. Roughly chop all of the nuts.

Combine the butter, vanilla extract and chocolate in a heatproof bowl. Sit on top of a saucepan of simmering water and melt the butter and chocolate. Remove the bowl once melted and cool to room temperature.

3

Preheat the oven to 150°C (130° fan) / 300F / gas 2. Grease and line a shallow square tin with greaseproof paper. In a bowl, whisk together the eggs and sugar until pale and fluffy.

4

Pour the cooled chocolate mixture on the egg and sugar mixture and fold together. Sift the flour and cocoa on top of this mixture and fold in gently.

5

Add the nuts and fold in. Pour into the tin and bake for 45 minutes.

6

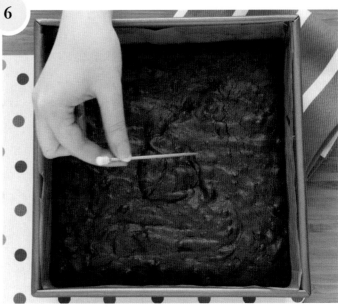

Remove from the oven and cool in the tin for 1 hour before turning out onto a chopping board. Cut into rectangles using a sharp knife.

Chocolate Shortbread

Ingredients

200 g / 7 oz / 1 ⅓ cups plain (all-purpose)
flour, sifted

30 g / 1 oz / 2 tbsp cocoa powder, sifted

150 g / 5 oz / ⅔ cup margarine, softened

75 g / 3 oz / ⅓ cup caster (superfine) sugar

1 tsp vanilla extract

1 tsp bicarbonate of (baking) soda

110 g / 4 oz / ½ cup marmalade

SERVES 24 | PREP TIME 10 minutes | COOKING TIME 25-30 minutes

Preheat the oven to 180°C (160° fan) / 350F / gas 4. Grease and line 2 baking trays with greaseproof paper. Prepare and measure all of the ingredients.

In a mixing bowl, cream together the margarine and sugar until pale and fluffy using an electric mixer.

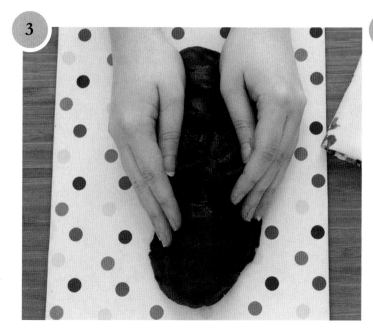

Beat in the flour, cocoa powder, bicarbonate of soda and vanilla extract and knead this dough lightly for 5 minutes.

Roll the dough into little balls, arranging on the baking tray and flattening a little before baking.

Bake for 15 minutes and let them cool on the tray for a few minutes before moving to a wire rack to cool completely.

Garnish each cookie with 1 tsp of marmalade before serving.

Herb Cakes

Ingredients

30 ml / 1 fl. oz / 2 tbsp sunflower oil

350 g / 12 oz / 2 ⅔ cups plain (all-purpose) flour, sifted

30 g / 1 oz / ¼ stick butter, melted

2 tsp baking powder

4 medium eggs

225 g / 8 oz / 2 cups Parmesan, finely grated

1 small bunch tarragon, finely chopped

1 small bunch flat-leaf parsley, finely chopped

salt and freshly ground black pepper

MAKES 8 | PREP TIME 15 minutes | COOKING TIME 25 minutes

Preheat the oven to 180°C (160° fan) / 350F / gas 4. Prepare and measure all of the ingredients.

Grease the base and sides of 8 small loaf tins.

In a large mixing bowl, beat the eggs until light and frothy.

Add the flour, melted butter, sunflower oil and baking powder and beat again until smooth.

Fold in the Parmesan and chopped herbs and season the batter well with salt and black pepper.

Spoon the batter into the prepared loaf tins. Bake for 25 minutes. Remove from the oven and allow them to cool in their tins. Serve warm or cold.

Blackberry and Raspberry Cakes

Ingredients

110 g / 4 oz / ½ cup caster (superfine) sugar

110 g / 4 oz / 1 stick unsalted butter, softened

a little extra butter, for greasing

75 g / 3 oz / ½ cup self-raising flour, sifted

30 g / 1 oz / 2 tbsp cornflour, sifted

30 g / 1 oz / 2 tbsp ground almonds

2 large eggs

2 tbsp milk

150 g / 5 oz / 1 ½ cup raspberries

150 g / 5 oz / 1 ½ cup blueberries

a pinch of salt

To garnish

2 tbsp icing (confectioner's) sugar

SERVES 8 | PREP TIME 15 minutes | COOKING TIME 20 minutes

Preheat the oven to 180°C (160° fan) / 350F / gas 4. Grease 8 brioche moulds with butter. Combine the sugar, butter, flour, cornflour, a pinch of salt and eggs in a bowl and beat for a few minutes until smooth and even.

Fold in the milk and almonds until incorporated, then add the raspberries and blueberries and fold them through as well.

Divide the batter evenly between the moulds and arrange them on baking trays.

Bake for 20 minutes until risen and golden; a toothpick should come out clean from their centres when they are done.

Remove from the oven and let the cakes cool on a wire rack. Dust with icing sugar once cool before serving.

Granary Bread

Ingredients

450 g / 1 lb / 3 cups wholemeal flour

300 g / 10 ½ oz / 2 cups strong plain flour

450 ml / 16 fl. oz / 2 cups warm water

55 ml / 2 fl. oz / ¼ cup tepid water

55ml / 2 fl. oz / ¼ cup sunflower oil

30 ml / 1 fl. oz / 2 tbsp honey

1 tbsp dried active yeast

½ tsp caster sugar

1 medium egg

1 tbsp lemon juice

2 tbsp flax seeds

2 tbsp sunflower seeds

2 tsp salt

MAKES 2 loaves | PREP TIME 15 minutes | COOKING TIME 45-50 minutes

Measure and prepare all of the ingredients.

In a bowl, combine the yeast and sugar with the water. In a separate large mixing bowl, combine the honey, oil, egg and lemon juice until smooth.

Add the yeast mixture to the larger bowl and mix stir well. Gradually add 300 g of the wholemeal flour, mixing well after each addition. Let the mixture stand to one side for 20 minutes, until very light.

Stir in the remaining wholemeal flour, strong plain flour and salt. Knead the dough on a lightly floured surface for 10-12 minutes until smooth, shiny and elastic and transfer to a greased bowl and cover. Let the dough rise for an hour in a warm place.

Remove from the bowl and punch down the dough. Shape into two loaves, cover and rest for 20 minutes. Preheat the oven to 190°C (170° fan) / 375F / gas 5. Transfer the loaves to a lightly greased tray and leave to rise for 20 minutes.

Brush the tops with a little water, then press the seeds into them. Bake for 25-35 minutes until they are light golden in colour. Transfer to a wire rack and allow to cool before serving.

Tomato Bread

Ingredients

550 g / 1 lb 4 oz / 3 ⅔ cups wholemeal flour

55 g / 2 oz / ½ stick butter, cubed

110 ml / 4 fl. oz / ½ cup whole milk

2 tbsp tomato puree

175 ml / 6 fl. oz / ¾ cup lukewarm water

3 tsp fast action dried yeast

2 tsp fine sea salt

55 g / 2 oz / ⅓ cup sun-dried tomatoes,
drained and finely chopped

MAKES 2 Loaves | PREP TIME 20-25 minutes | COOKING TIME 40-45 minutes

Combine the flour, salt and yeast in a large mixing bowl.

Rub the butter into the flour mixture using your fingertips until it resembles fine breadcrumbs.

Combine the warm milk, tomato puree and water in a jug, whisking well until smooth. Pour into the flour mixture, mixing well with a wooden spoon until you have a soft dough.

Add the chopped sun-dried tomato and work this into the dough. Turn out onto a lightly floured work surface and knead for 10-15 minutes until you have a smooth, elastic dough. Place the dough in a large mixing bowl and cover with a damp tea towel.

Leave the dough to rise in a warm place. After 1 hour remove from the bowl and knock it down using your hands. Divide into 2 even portions and shape into rounds. .

Place them on oiled baking trays and cover with oiled film, leaving them to rise for 1 hour. Preheat the oven to 190°C (170°C fan) / 375F / gas 5. Remove the film and bake for 25-30 minutes until risen. Remove from the oven and let them cool on wire racks before serving.

Sweetcorn Bread

Ingredients

450 g / 1 lb / 3 cups wholemeal flour

300 g / 10 ½ oz / 2 cups strong plain flour

450 ml / 16 fl. oz / 2 cups warm water

55 ml / 2 fl. oz / ¼ cup tepid water

55 ml / 2 fl. oz / ¼ cup sunflower oil

30 ml / 1 fl. oz / 2 tbsp honey

1 tbsp dried active yeast

½ tsp caster (superfine) sugar

1 small egg

225 g / 8 oz / 1 cup canned sweetcorn, drained

110 ml / 4 fl. oz / ½ cup whole milk, warmed

MAKES 2 loaves | PREP TIME 15 minutes | COOKING TIME 45-50 minutes

Prepare and measure all of the ingredients. Blitz the sweetcorn in a food processor with the warm milk until smooth. Press the mixture through a sieve, collecting the sweetcorn puree in a bowl beneath.

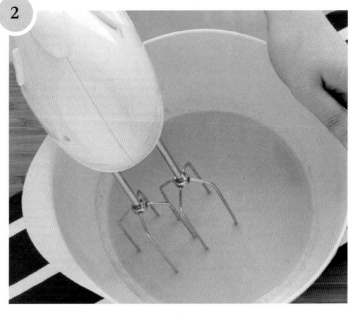

In a bowl, combine the yeast and sugar with the tepid water. In a separate large bowl, combine the honey, oil, egg and sweetcorn puree, whisking until smooth.

3

Add the yeast mixture to the larger bowl and mix stir well. Gradually add 300 g of the wholemeal flour, mixing well after each addition. Let the mixture stand to one side for 20 minutes, until very light.

4

Stir in the remaining flour and salt until the dough starts to come away from the sides of the bowl. Knead the dough on a lightly floured surface for 10 minutes until smooth and elastic, then transfer to a greased bowl and cover.

5

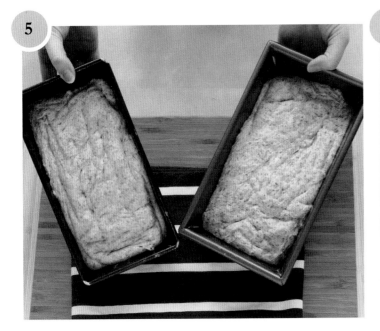

Let the dough rise in a warm place. After 1 hour, remove from the bowl and punch down. Shape into 2 loaves, cover and leave to rise for 20 minutes. Preheat the oven to 190°C (170° fan) / 375F / gas 5. Transfer the loaves to lightly-greased tins and leave to rise for 20 minutes.

6

Bake for 25-35 minutes until the bottom of the loaves sound hollow and their tops are light golden brown colour. Transfer to a wire rack and allow to cool before slicing and serving.

Small Breads

Ingredients

500 g / 1 lb 2 oz / 3 ⅓ cups strong white
bread flour

extra bread flour, for dusting

30 g / 1 oz / ¼ stick butter, cubed

75 ml / 3 fl. oz / ⅓ cup whole milk

225 ml / 8 fl. oz / 1 cup lukewarm water

2 tsp fast action dried yeast

1 tsp salt

SERVES 12 | PREP TIME 15 minutes | COOKING TIME 18 minutes

Prepare and measure all of the ingredients. Slice the butter into small chunks.

Combine the flour, salt and yeast in a bowl. Rub the butter into the flour mixture using your fingertips. Combine the milk and water in a jug and pour into the mixture, mixing well until you have a soft dough.

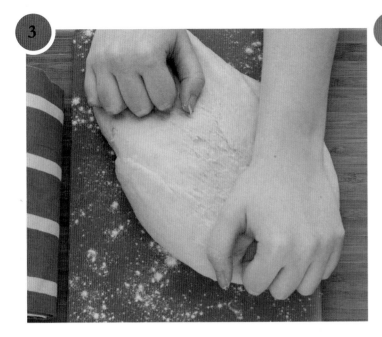

Turn out onto a floured work surface and knead for 10 minutes until smooth. Place in a bowl and cover with a damp cloth. Leave to rise in a warm place. After 1 hour, remove and knock it down using your hands.

Divide into 12 and place in the holes of a lightly greased muffin tin.

Make cross-shaped incisions in their tops using a sharp paring knife.

Cover with a piece of oiled film and leave to rise in a warm place for 1 hour. Preheat the oven to 200°C (180° fan) / 400F / gas 6. Bake for 18 minutes. Remove and dust with a little flour before cooling on a wire rack.

Walnut and Cheese Loaf

Ingredients

450 g / 1 lb / 3 cups strong wholemeal bread flour

a little extra wholemeal flour, for dusting

150 g / 5 oz / 1 cup strong white bread flour

110 g / 4 oz / ⅔ cup walnuts

1 tbsp caster (superfine) sugar

1 tsp salt

3 tsp dried active yeast

3 tbsp walnut oil

425 ml / 15 fl. oz / 1 ¾ cups warm water

55 g / 2 oz / ½ cup Cheddar, grated

55 g / 2 oz / ½ cup Gruyere, grated

MAKES 2 | PREP TIME 10 minutes | COOKING TIME 35 minutes

Prepare and measure all of the ingredients. Finely grind the walnuts in a food processor then transfer them to a bowl.

Sift together the flours, salt and sugar in a bowl. Add the ground walnuts and stir well to combine. Sprinkle over the yeast, then pour in the warm water and oil. Bring together into a dough.

3

Turn out onto a floured surface and knead for 10 minutes until smooth. Cover with a damp cloth and leave to rise in a warm place. After 1 hour, knock the dough back and knead for 5 more minutes.

4

Grease 2 baking trays and divide the dough in half. Shape into rough loaf shapes. Cover with a damp cloth towel and leave to rise for 30 minutes.

5

Preheat the oven to 180°C (160° fan) / 350F / gas 4. Bake for 35 minutes until golden. Remove from the oven and transfer to a wire rack for 2 minutes.

6

Sprinkle the tops with the cheeses. Return to the oven for 5 minutes until the cheese melts. Remove from the oven and let them cool on wire racks before serving.

Spinach Savoury Cake

Ingredients

250 g / 9 oz / 1 ⅔ cups self-raising flour, sifted

125 ml / 4 ½ fl. oz / ½ cup olive oil

110 g / 4 oz / 1 cup Parmesan, finely grated

2 large eggs, beaten

225 g / 8 oz / 2 cups spinach, washed and chopped

55 g / 2 oz / ¼ cup pine nuts, toasted

salt and pepper

SERVES 8 | PREP TIME 10-15 minutes | COOKING TIME 55 minutes

Preheat the oven to 170°C (150° fan) / 325F / gas 3. Prepare and measure all of the ingredients.

Blanch the spinach in a large saucepan of boiling, salted water for 15 seconds. Drain in a colander and let it cool to one side.

Combine all the remaining ingredients apart from the pine nuts in a large bowl and blend until smooth.

Add the spinach and blitz using a blender until the spinach is broken up. Add most of the pine nuts to the mixture and fold through, reserving the remaining pine nuts for a garnish.

Spoon the batter into the tin and bake for 55 minutes. Remove from the oven and let it cool in the tin for 15-20 minutes.

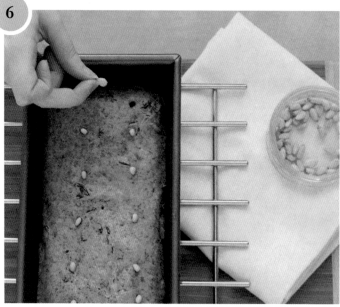

Stud the top of the cake with the remaining pine nuts then turn out onto a wire rack and leave to cool before serving.

Cheese Sticks

Ingredients

320 g / 11 oz / 2 sheets ready-made
puff pastry

a little plain (all-purpose) flour, for dusting

225 g / 8 oz / 2 cups Gruyere, finely grated

4 tsp cumin seeds, lightly crushed

salt and ground black pepper

MAKES 16 | PREP TIME 10-15 minutes | COOKING TIME 12 minutes

Pre-heat the oven to 220°C (200° fan) / 425F / gas 7. Prepare and measure all of the ingredients and grate the cheese.

Roll the pastry out on a lightly floured surface into a large square.

Sprinkle half the cheese and half of the cumin on top, then fold the pastry over in half.

Roll out to a rectangle with 0.5 cm thickness. Cut into 2 cm wide strips and then twist 4-5 times.

Carefully arrange on lined baking trays, spaced apart.

Sprinkle over the remaining cheese and cumin, along with some seasoning. Bake for 12 minutes until golden in colour. Remove and cool on a wire rack before serving.

Poppy Seed Loaf

Ingredients

600 g / 1 lb 5 oz / 4 cups strong white bread
flour

110 g / 4 oz / ⅔ cup wholemeal flour

extra bread flour, for dusting

2 tsp dried yeast

1 tsp salt

1 tsp sugar

1 tbsp olive oil

55 ml / 2 fl. oz / ¼ cup whole milk

450 ml / 16 fl. oz / 2 cups warm water

55 g / 2 oz / ⅓ cup poppy seeds

SERVES 2 | PREP TIME 15 minutes | COOKING TIME 50 minutes

Prepare and measure all of the ingredients. Sift the flour into a large bowl.

Combine the flours, sugar, salt and yeast in a bowl, then work the olive oil in. dd the warm water steadily until you can form a sticky dough.

3

Turn out onto a floured surface and knead for 10 minutes until smooth.

4

Place in a bowl and cover with film. Leave to rise in a warm for 1 hour.

5

Grease 2 baking trays. Turn the dough, knock it back and knead for 3 minutes. Divide in two and shape into rounds. Cover with oiled film and leave for 40 minutes. Preheat the oven to 220°C (200° fan) / 425F / gas 7.

6

Brush the top of each round with warm water, then press the poppy seeds into the tops. Make a cross-shaped incision in the top of each round and bake for 40 minutes. Remove and let the bread cool on wire racks.

Small Bread Loaves

Ingredients

900 g / 2 lb / 6 cups strong plain white flour

a little flour, for dusting

4 tsp fast action dried yeast

1 tsp caster (superfine) sugar

1 tsp salt

55 g / 2 oz / ½ stick butter, cubed

150 ml / 5 fl. oz / ⅔ cup whole milk, warmed

450 ml / 16 fl. oz / 2 cups lukewarm water

SERVES 12 | PREP TIME 10 minutes | COOKING TIME 40-45 minutes

Combine the flour, salt and dried yeast in a large mixing bowl.

Rub the butter into the flour using your fingertips until you have a mixture resembling fine breadcrumbs.

3

Combine the warm milk and water in a jug and pour into the flour mixture, mixing well with a wooden spoon until you have a soft dough. Turn out onto a lightly floured surface and knead for 10 minutes until you have a smooth, elastic dough.

4

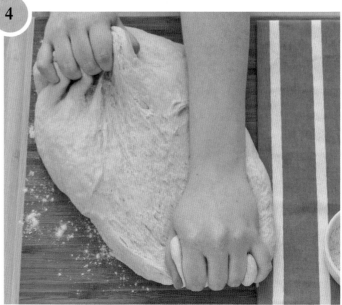

Place the dough in a large bowl and cover with a damp tea towel. Leave the dough to rise in a warm place until doubled in size. After proving and doubling in size, remove the dough from the bowl and knock it down using your hands.

5

Divide the dough into 12 even balls and shape into small loaf shapes. Arrange on a oiled baking trays and cover with pieces of oiled film, leaving them to prove in a warm place until doubled in size again.

6

Preheat the oven to 220°C (200°C fan) / 425F / gas 7. Remove the film when ready to bake and bake the rolls for 8-10 minutes until golden and risen. Remove from the oven and leave to cool on a wire rack before serving.

Gouda Loaf

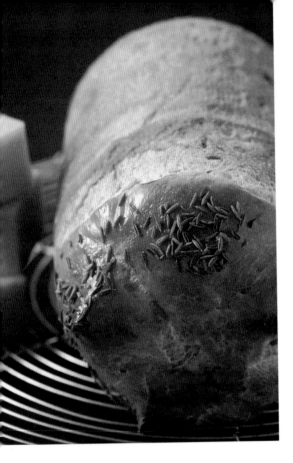

Ingredients

550 g / 1 lb 4 oz / 3 ⅔ cups strong bread flour

55 g / 2 oz / ½ stick butter, cubed

110 ml / 4 fl. oz / ½ cup whole milk

175 ml / 6 fl. oz / ¾ cup lukewarm water

3 tsp fast action dried yeast

2 tsp fine sea salt

110 g / 4 oz / 1 cup Gouda, grated

1 tbsp cumin seeds, lightly crushed

To garnish

110 g / 4 oz / 1 cup Gouda, cut into chunks

1 tsp honey

1 tbsp cumin seeds

MAKES 2 | PREP TIME 10-15 minutes | COOKING TIME 40-50 minutes

1 Prepare and measure all of the ingredients. Combine the flour, salt and yeast in a large mixing bowl.

2 Rub the butter into the flour until it resembles fine breadcrumbs. Combine the warm milk and water in a jug, whisking well. Pour into the flour mixture, mixing well with a wooden spoon until you have a soft dough.

3

Add the Gouda and half of the cumin seeds and work them into the dough. Turn out onto a lightly floured work surface and knead for 10-15 minutes until you have a smooth, elastic dough.

4

Place the dough in a bowl and cover with a damp cloth. Leave to rise in a warm place. After 1 hour, knock it down using your hands. Divide into 2 even portions and shape into two hinged bread pans.

5

Leave them to prove for 1 hour until doubled in size, making sure you leave the pans open. Preheat the oven to 190°C (170° fan) / 375F / gas 5.

6

Close the pans and bake for 30 minutes. Remove from the oven and let them cool on wire racks before brushing one end of each with honey. Sprinkle the cumin seeds for the garnish on top of the honey so they stick. Serve on wire racks garnished with Gouda.

Rosemary Focaccia

Ingredients

250 g / 9 oz / 1 ⅔ cups strong white
bread flour
a little bread flour, for dusting
150 ml / 5 fl. oz / ⅔ cup tepid water
1 tsp dried yeast
30 ml / 1 fl. oz / 2 tbsp olive oil
3 sprigs of rosemary
1 tsp fine sea salt

SERVES 8 | PREP TIME 10 minutes | COOKING TIME 25-30 minutes

Prepare and measure all of the ingredients. Remove the leaves from the stems of the rosemary and chop finely.

Combine 25 ml of the water with the yeast and leave in a small bowl for 5 minutes to dissolve.

3

Combine the flour and salt in a bowl, making a well in the centre. Add the yeast and water mixture and the olive oil, mixing thoroughly until combined. Gradually add the remaining water to the mixture, mixing until you have a dough.

4

Turn the dough out onto a lightly floured surface and knead for 8-10 minutes until you have a smooth, elastic dough.

5

Form the dough into a ball and rest in a lightly oiled bowl. Cover with a damp tea towel and leave to rise in a warm place for 1 hour. Once risen, knock the dough back and place in the bowl. Cover and leave to rise for 20-30 minutes.

6

Knock the dough back and knead for a few minutes. Preheat the oven to 190°C (170° fan) / 375F / gas 5. Divide the dough into 2 balls and roll out into squares. Sprinkle the rosemary on top and bake for 15-20 minutes until golden. Remove from the oven and garnish with salt before serving.

Olive Bread Sticks

Ingredients

For the dough

900 g / 2 lbs / 6 cups plain (all-purpose)
flour

a little plain (all-purpose) flour, for dusting

3 tsp active dry yeast

700 ml / 1 pint 5 fl. oz / 3 cups warm water

110 ml / 4 fl. oz / ½ cup olive oil

110 ml / 4 fl. oz / ½ cup extra-virgin olive oil

2 tsp sea salt

For the fillings

225 g / 8 oz / 1 cup pitted black olives,
drained

225 g / 8 oz / 2 cups Parma ham, chopped

MAKES 4 rolls | PREP TIME 15 minutes | COOKING TIME 45-55 minutes

Prepare and measure all of the ingredients. Pour the water into a large bowl and add the yeast. Allow it to dissolve then mix in 225 g of flour and the olive oil until smooth. Keep adding 225 g of the flour at a time until a tacky dough forms.

Divide the dough in two and knead the olives into one part of the dough. Knead the Parma ham into the other half of the dough.

90

Turn the doughs out onto a lightly floured surface and knead until smooth and elastic. Transfer the doughs to lightly oiled bowls and cover with a damp cloth. Leave them to rise in a warm place for 60 minutes before turning out and punching down.

Shape the doughs into 4 flat ovals. Lightly oil the baking sheets with 1 tbsp of extra-virgin olive oil and transfer the dough to them. Cover with a damp cloth and allow to prove for a further 20 minutes.

Meanwhile, preheat the oven to 190°C (170° fan) / 375F / gas 5. Make three deep incisions all the way through each piece of dough, spaced apart evenly.

Place a small tray of water in the base of the oven and bake the doughs for 20-25 minutes until golden. Remove and brush with the remaining extra-virgin olive oil. Allow to cool completely on a wire rack before serving.

Walnut Bread

Ingredients

600 g / 1 lb 5 oz / 4 cups strong wholemeal
bread flour

extra flour, for dusting

110 g / 4 oz / ⅔ cup walnuts, finely chopped

450 ml / 16 fl. oz / 2 cups warm water

55 ml / 2 fl. oz / ¼ cup walnut oil

4 tsp dried active yeast

1 tbsp caster (superfine) sugar

1 tsp salt

MAKES 1 | PREP TIME 10 minutes | COOKING TIME 40-50 minutes

Prepare and measure all of the ingredients. Finely chop the walnuts.

Sift together the flour, salt and sugar in a large mixing bowl.

Add the walnuts, stir well to combine and sprinkle over the yeast.

Pour in the water and oil. Combine into a dough using your hands, then turn out onto a floured surface and knead for 10 minutes, until you have a smooth, elastic dough.

Cover with a damp cloth and leave to prove in a warm place for 1 hour. Knock the dough back and knead for 5 minutes on a lightly floured surface. Shape the dough into an oval shape.

Grease a tray and place the dough on it. Cover with the cloth and leave to rise for 30 minutes. Preheat the oven to 190°C (170°C fan) / 375F / gas 5. Bake for 40 minutes until risen. Allow to cool on a wire rack before serving.

Parmesan and Basil Rolls

Ingredients

110 g / 4 oz / ⅔ cup plain (all-purpose) flour, sifted

plain (all-purpose) flour, for dusting

55 g / 2 oz / ½ cup Parmesan, grated

55 g / 2 oz / ½ stick unsalted butter, melted

1 medium egg yolk

2 tsp dried basil

½ tsp salt

30 g / 1 oz / 4 tbsp basil leaves

MAKES 24 | PREP TIME 10 minutes | COOKING TIME 25-30 minutes

Prepare and measure all of the ingredients. Wash the basil leaves and grate the Parmesan cheese.

Combine the flour, butter, Parmesan, dried basil and salt in a food processor. Pulse until the mixture resembles fine breadcrumbs.

3

Add the egg yolk and pulse again until the mixture comes together to form a dough; add a little warm water if the dough is too dry.

4

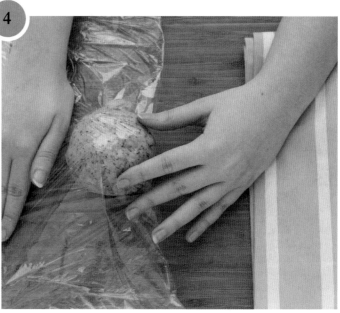

Turn the mixture out onto a work surface and form into a ball. Wrap in cling film and chill for 15 minutes. Preheat the oven to 180°C (160° fan) / 350F / gas 4.

5

Grease and line a couple of baking trays with greaseproof paper. Remove the dough from the fridge and roll out on a lightly floured work surface to 1 cm thickness.

6

Use a 3-4 cm cutter to punch out rounds of the dough. Place carefully onto the trays and decorate each with a basil leaf. Bake for 10 minutes. Remove from the oven and let them cool before serving.

Courgette and Rosemary Focaccias

Ingredients

250 g / 9 oz / 1 ⅔ cups strong white
bread flour
a little bread flour, for dusting
150 ml / 5 fl. oz / ⅔ cup tepid water
1 tsp dried yeast
30 ml / 1 fl. oz / 2 tbsp olive oil

3 sprigs of rosemary, leaves stripped from
their stems and very finely chopped
1 tsp fine sea salt
1 large courgette, finely sliced
2 tsp flaked sea salt

SERVES 8 | PREP TIME 10 minutes | COOKING TIME 25-30 minutes

Prepare and measure all of the ingredients. Strip the leaves from the stems of the rosemary and set to one side.

Combine 25 ml of the water with the yeast and leave in a small bowl for 5 minutes. Combine the flour and salt in a large bowl, making a well in the centre. Add the water mix and olive oil, mixing thoroughly until combined.

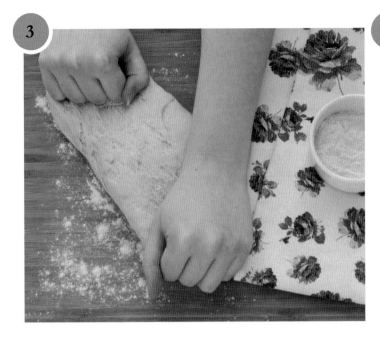

Gradually add the remaining water, mixing until you have a dough. Turn the dough out onto a floured surface and knead for 8-10 minutes. Form into a ball and rest in a lightly oiled bowl. Cover with a damp tea towel and leave to rise in a warm place for 1 hour.

Once risen, knock the dough back and transfer back to the bowl. Cover and leave to rise for 25 minutes. Knock the dough back, and then knead for a few minutes.

Preheat the oven to 190°C (170°C fan) / 375F / gas 5. Divide the dough into 5 even balls and roll out into rounds. Arrange the sliced courgette on top in overlapping slices.

Sprinkle the rosemary on top and bake for 15-20 minutes until golden and risen. Remove from the oven and garnish with the sea salt before serving.

Cheese Loaf

Ingredients

350 g / 12 oz / 2 ⅓ cups plain (all-purpose)
flour, sifted

30 ml / 1 fl. oz / 2 tbsp sunflower oil

30 g / 1 oz / ¼ stick butter, melted

2 tsp baking powder

4 medium eggs

110 g / 4 oz / 1 cup Parmesan, finely grated

110 g / 4 oz / 1 cup Gruyere, finely grated

½ tsp salt

SERVES 4 | PREP TIME 10-15 minutes | COOKING TIME 20-25 minutes

Preheat the oven to 170°C (150°C fan) /325F / gas 3. Prepare and measure all of the ingredients.

Grease and line a 6" square cake tin with greaseproof paper.

In a large mixing bowl, beat the eggs until light and frothy.

Add the flour, salt, melted butter, sunflower oil and baking powder and beat again until smooth.

Fold in the Parmesan and most of the Gruyere, keeping a small handful behind for garnishing.

Spoon the batter into the tin and bake for 15-20 minutes. Remove from the oven and sprinkle the remaining cheese on top. Let it cool for 15 minutes before moving to a wire rack to finish cooling.

Cheese Scones

Ingredients

30 ml / 1 fl. oz / 2 tbsp sunflower oil

350 g / 12 oz / 2 ⅓ cups plain (all-purpose) flour, sifted

2 tsp baking powder

30 g /1 oz / ¼ stick butter, melted

4 medium eggs

225 g / 8 oz / 2 cups Roquefort, crumbled

salt and freshly ground black pepper

MAKES 6-8 | PREP TIME 10 minutes | COOKING TIME 25 minutes

Preheat the oven to 180°C (160° fan) / 350F / gas 4. Prepare and measure all of the ingredients.

In a bowl, beat the eggs together until light and frothy.

3

Add the flour, melted butter, sunflower oil and baking powder and beat again until smooth.

4

Fold in the crumbled Roquefort and season the batter well with salt and black pepper.

5

Spoon into assorted individual loaf tins. Bake for 25 minutes until a skewer comes out clean from their centres.

6

Remove from the oven and allow to cool in their tins for 5 minutes, before turning out onto a wire rack to cool completely. Serve warm or cold.

Sesame Seed Rolls

Ingredients

500 g / 1 lb 2 oz / 3 ⅓ cups wholemeal flour

a little plain (all-purpose) flour, for dusting

30 g / 1 oz / ¼ stick butter, cubed

75 ml / 3 fl. oz / ⅓ cup whole milk

225 ml / 8 fl. oz / 1 cup lukewarm water

2 tsp fast action dried yeast

1 tsp salt

To garnish

55 ml / 2 fl. oz / ¼ cup whole milk

55 g / 2 oz / ½ cup sesame seeds

MAKES 4 rolls | PREP TIME 20 minutes | COOKING TIME 25-30 minutes

Measure and prepare all of the ingredients. Combine the flour, salt and yeast in a large mixing bowl.

Rub the butter into the flour mixture using your fingertips until it resembles fine breadcrumbs. Combine the warm milk and water in a jug and pour into the flour mixture, mixing well with a wooden spoon until you have a soft dough.

Turn out onto a lightly floured work surface and knead for 10-15 minutes until you have a smooth, elastic dough. Place the dough in a large mixing bowl and cover with a damp tea towel.

Leave the dough to rise in a warm place until doubled in size; roughly 1 hour. After doubling in size, remove the dough from the bowl and knock it down using your hands.

Divide into 4 even portions and shape into rough flute shapes. Space them apart on oiled baking trays and make diagonal indents in their tops using a sharp knife.

Cover with film and leave to prove in a warm place for 1 hour. Preheat the oven to 200°C (180° fan) / 400F / gas 6. Bake for 14-18 minutes until risen. Remove from the oven, brush their tops with the milk and sprinkle their tops with sesame seeds.

Mocha Cake

Ingredients

110 g / 4 oz / 1 stick unsalted butter, softened

110 g / 4 oz / ⅔ cup self-raising flour, sifted

110 g / 4 oz / ½ cup caster (superfine) sugar

2 large eggs

55 ml / 2 fl. oz / ¼ cup whole milk

55 g / 2 oz / ⅓ cup cocoa powder, sifted

2 tsp coffee granules

30 ml / 1 fl. oz / 2 tbsp boiling water

Buttercream icing and garnish

55 g / 2 oz / ½ stick butter, softened

125 g / 4 ½ oz / 1 cup icing (confectioner's) sugar, sifted

30 g / 1 oz / 2 tbsp cocoa powder, sifted

1 tsp instant coffee granules

1 tbsp boiling water

55 g / 2 oz / ⅓ cup dark chocolate, grated

SERVES 2 | PREP TIME 30 minutes | COOKING TIME 25 minutes

Pre-heat the oven to 170°C (150° fan) / 325F / gas 3. Prepare and measure all of the ingredients.

In a bowl, combine the butter, sugar, eggs, self-raising flour, cocoa powder together and mix until smooth.

3

Mix the coffee granules with the hot water to form a thin paste and stir this into the cake batter.

4

Pour the batter into a square greased and lined cake tin and bake in the oven for 25 minutes. Remove from the oven and let the cake cool for a few minutes before turning out and cooling on a wire rack.

5

Meanwhile, combine the butter, the icing sugar and the cocoa powder in a bowl until smooth. Combine the coffee granules and hot water to form a thin paste and combine with the buttercream icing.

6

Once cool, cut the cake in half vertically. Spread the cake with the buttercream icing on the top and sides and use the grated chocolate to decorate the sides of the cake.

7

Cut the cake in half and use a fork to create a wave pattern on the top and pipe any unused icing on top at the corners of the squares of cake before serving.

Chocolate Pudding

Ingredients

For the chocolate puddings

30 g / 1 oz / ¼ stick butter, melted

75 g / 2 ¾ oz / ½ cup plain (all-purpose) flour, sifted

30 g / 1 oz / ¼ cup ground almonds

110 g / 4 oz / ⅔ cup good-quality dark chocolate, chopped

110 g / 4 oz / 1 stick unsalted butter, cubed

2 tbsp cocoa powder, sifted

2 medium eggs

2 medium egg yolks

For the cookies

110 g / 4 oz / ⅔ cup plain (all-purpose) flour, sifted

110 g / 4 oz / ⅔ cup dark chocolate, chopped

75 g / 3 oz / ¾ stick unsalted butter, cubed

55 g / 2 oz / ⅓ cup icing (confectioner's) sugar

55 g / 2 oz / ⅓ cup good quality cocoa powder, sifted

½ tsp vanilla extract

½ tsp salt

1 medium egg

SERVES 4 | PREP TIME 20 minutes | COOKING TIME 80 minutes

Prepare and measure all of the ingredients.

Start preparing the cookie dough by combining together the icing sugar, cocoa powder, flour and salt in a bowl. Rub the butter into this mixture until it resembles fine breadcrumbs.

3

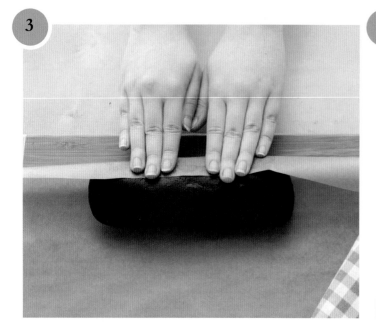

Add the egg, dark chocolate and vanilla extract and mix until a stiff dough forms. Gather up and roll into a sausage shape with a diameter of 7-8 cm. Wrap in greaseproof paper and chill in the fridge for at least 30 minutes.

4

Grease and line a tray with greaseproof paper. Preheat the oven to 180°C (160° fan) / 350F / gas 4. Cut 1cm thick cookies out of the dough. Place on the tray and bake for 12-14 minutes. Remove and leave to cool for 10 minutes before moving to a wire rack to cool completely. Place in an airtight container and seal until ready to serve.

5

Brush 4 ovenproof glass ramekins with some of the melted butter. Chill the ramekins for 15 minutes, then brush with another layer of butter. Dust the insides with cocoa powder.

6

7

Chill until ready to fill with the batter. Increase the oven to 200°C / (180° fan) / 400F / gas 6. Melt together the chocolate and cubed butter in a heatproof bowl set over a pan of gently simmering water. Once melted, remove from the heat and allow to cool for 10 minutes.

Meanwhile, whisk together the eggs and egg yolks in a separate bowl until light and thick. Sift the plain flour into the eggs and whisk until smooth, then fold in the ground almonds until combined.

8

Pour the chocolate into the batter a bit at a time, mixing well. Divide the batter between the ramekins and place on a baking sheet. Bake in the oven for 10-12 minutes until the tops are set. Remove from the oven and leave to cool for a few minutes before serving with the cookies.

Chocolate Fudge Cake

Ingredients

For the cake

110 g / 4 oz / ⅔ cup dark chocolate

110 g / 4 oz / 1 stick unsalted butter, softened

175 g / 6 oz / ⅔ cup caster (superfine) sugar

75 g / 3 oz / ½ cup self-raising flour, sifted

75 g / 3 oz / ⅔ cup ground almonds

3 medium egg yolks

3 medium egg whites

a pinch of salt

2 tbsp dark rum

¼ tsp almond extract

To garnish

160 g / 5 oz / 1 cup dark chocolates

110 g / 4 oz / 1 stick unsalted butter, softened

2 tbsp dark rum

1 tbsp glucose syrup

SERVES 8 | PREP TIME 15 minutes | COOKING TIME 50-60 minutes

Preheat the oven to 180°C (160° fan) / 350F / gas 4. Grease and line a 7" tin. Place the chocolate and rum in a heatproof bowl set over a saucepan of simmering water. Stir until melted then remove from the heat.

Cream together the butter and sugar in a bowl, beating until pale and fluffy. Add the egg yolks and beat well until incorporated.

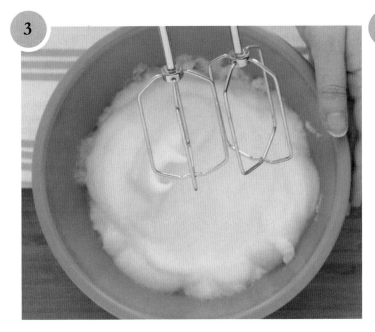

Whisk the egg whites with a pinch of salt in a separate bowl until they form soft peaks.

Add the chocolate to the butter and sugar mix. Add the almonds, almond extract and flour and fold through. Add ⅓ of the egg whites and whisk well. Add the remaining egg whites and fold through gently.

Spoon the mix into the tin and bake for 30 minutes. Remove from the oven and let it cool for 10 minutes. Remove from the tin and let it cool on a wire rack. Once the cake is cool, prepare the icing.

Combine the chocolate, rum, glucose and butter in a bowl and place on a saucepan of simmering water, stirring until smooth. Remove and cool for 10 minutes. Place the cake on a plate and pour the icing on top, covering the cake entirely.

Bilberry Pie

Ingredients

160 g / 5 ½ oz / 1 sheet shortcrust pastry
plain (all-purpose) flour, for dusting
600 g 1 lb 5 oz / 4 cups bilberries
(use blueberries if not available)
150 g / 5 oz / ⅔ cup caster (superfine) sugar
1 lemon, juiced
1 small egg, beaten

To garnish

225 ml / 8 fl. oz / 1 cup double cream
2 tbsp icing (confectioner's) sugar
55 g / 2 oz / ⅓ cup blueberries

SERVES 6 | PREP TIME 15 minutes | COOKING TIME 70 minutes

Combine the cornflour, bilberries, lemon juice and sugar (apart from 1 tbsp) in a large mixing bowl. Cover and let stand for 15 minutes.

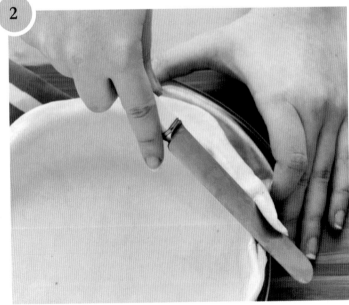

Preheat the oven to 180°C (160° fan) / 350F / gas 4. Roll the pastry out on a lightly floured surface to 1 cm thickness. Line a 9" ceramic pie plate with the pastry, cutting off the overhanging pastry.

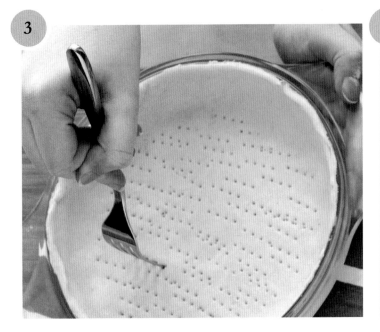

Prick the base all over with a fork. Gather the excess pastry into a ball and roll out to 0.5 cm thickness and reserve to one side.

Fill the pastry with the blueberry mixture. Cut the pastry into long strips that will act as decoration across the top of the pie.

Arrange in a wide lattice pattern making sure each strip of pastry reaches the edge of the pie plate.

Seal well and brush the pastry with the beaten egg. Bake for 45-50 minutes. Remove and leave to rest for a few minutes. Whip the cream and icing sugar together in a bowl until soft peaks form. Spoon into a serving bowl and serve alongside the pie and the blueberries for the garnish.

Chocolate and Walnut Sponge

Ingredients

For the sponge cake

110 g / 4 oz / ⅔ cup plain (all-purpose) flour

30 g / 1 oz / 2 tbsp cocoa powder

110 g / 4 oz / ½ cup golden caster (superfine) sugar

110 ml / 4 fl. oz / ½ cup sunflower oil

55 g / 2 oz / ⅓ cup dark chocolate, chopped

55 g / 2 oz / ⅓ cup walnuts

2 large eggs

1 ½ tsp baking powder

1 tsp vanilla extract

a pinch of salt

To garnish

110 g / 4 oz / ⅔ cup dark chocolate, chopped

1 tsp glucose syrup

4 walnut halves

SERVES 8 | PREP TIME 10-15 minutes | COOKING TIME 40-45 minutes

1

Prepare and measure all of the ingredients. Preheat the oven to 170°C (150° fan) / 325F / gas 3. Grease a 12" yule log mould with cooking spray.

2

Blitz the walnuts in a food processor until very fine. Transfer to a bowl and sift in the flour, cocoa powder, baking powder and salt. Stir well, then add the remaining ingredients for the cake and beat with an electric mixer for a couple of minutes until smooth, scraping down the sides from time to time.

3

Spoon the batter into the mould and bake for 18-25 minutes. Remove from the oven when ready and let the cake cool for 10 minutes.

4

Turn out onto a wire rack to finish cooling.

5

Combine the chocolate and glucose syrup in a small heatproof bowl. Set the bowl on top of a saucepan of gently simmering water, stirring occasionally, until melted and smooth.

6

Remove the bowl from the heat and let it cool for a few minutes. Place the cake with the flat side down on a serving plate and pour the melted chocolate along its spine. Garnish with the 4 walnut halves in a row on top.

Carrot and Cinnamon Cake

Ingredients

450 g / 1 lb / 2 cups carrots, peeled
and grated

150 g / 5 oz / 1 ½ sticks unsalted butter

150 g / 5 oz / 1 cup self-raising flour, sifted

110 ml / 4 fl. oz / ⅓ cup golden syrup

55 g / 2 oz / ⅓ cup soft light brown sugar

3 medium eggs

2 tsp ground cinnamon

½ tsp ground nutmeg

a pinch of salt

SERVES 8 | PREP TIME 15 minutes | COOKING TIME 70 minutes

Prepare and measure all of the ingredients. Preheat the oven to 170°C (150° fan) / 325F / gas 3. Grease and line a loaf tin with greaseproof paper.

Combine the butter, flour, sugar, golden syrup, eggs, ground spices and salt in a large mixing bowl and beat using an electric mixer until smooth.

3

Add the grated carrot and fold through until incorporated.

4

Spoon into the prepared loaf tin and bake for 50-60 minutes until a cake tester comes out clean from the centre.

5

Remove from the oven and let it cool in the tin for 20 minutes before turning out onto a wire rack to finish cooling. Peel off any greaseproof paper before serving.

Pineapple Coconut Tart

Ingredients

160 g / 5 ½ oz / 1 sheet ready-made
shortcrust pastry

plain (all-purpose) flour, for dusting

900 g / 2 lbs / 4 cups canned pineapple
rings, drained

75 g / 3 oz / ¾ cup desiccated coconut

75 g / 3 oz / ⅓ cup caster (superfine) sugar

2 tbsp white rum

2 tbsp apricot jam, warmed

SERVES 8 | PREP TIME 10 minutes | COOKING TIME 25 minutes

Preheat the oven to 180°C (160°) / 350F / gas 4. Prepare and measure all of the ingredients.

Roll the pastry out on a floured surface to 0.5 cm thickness. Use it to line an 8" tart tin, pressing the pastry into the edges and letting any excess pastry overhand the sides of the tin.

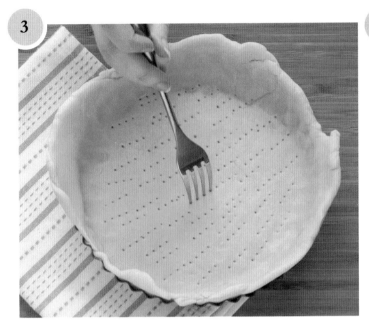

Prick the base all over with a fork and chill for 10 minutes.

Combine the pineapple rings, rum, sugar and half of the rum in a bowl, tossing well to combine. Remove the pastry after 10 minutes and layer the pineapple rings inside the pastry.

Bake for 25 minutes until the pastry is cooked and golden in appearance. Remove from the oven and let it cool on a wire rack for 5 minutes before trimming the excess pastry using a sharp, serrated knife.

Carefully turn the tart out onto a serving plate and sprinkle the top with the remaining desiccated coconut before serving.

Italian Rice Tart

Ingredients

200 g / 7 oz / 1 cup arborio rice

450 ml / 16 fl. oz / 2 cups whole milk

450 g / 1 lb / 2 cups caster (superfine) sugar

450 g / 1 lb / 2 cups ricotta, drained

7 large eggs

110 g / 4 oz / ½ cup hazelnuts (cob nuts),
roughly chopped

½ lemon, juiced

2 tsp vanilla extract

SERVES 8 | PREP TIME 10-15 minutes | COOKING TIME 80 minutes

Prepare and measure all of the ingredients. Preheat the oven to 180°C (160° fan) / 350F / gas 4.

Combine the rice and milk in a large saucepan and heat until it starts to boil. Reduce the heat and cook the rice uncovered for 15 minutes, stirring frequently, until the rice has absorbed the milk. Remove the saucepan from the heat and set it to one side.

3

Beat the eggs and sugar together in a large mixing bowl using an electric mixer until they are well combined and the sugar has dissolved.

4

Add the lemon juice and vanilla extract and stir a few times.

5

Fold this mixture into the eggs and sugar using a spatula, until thoroughly combined. Add the hazelnut and fold them into the mixture.

6

Grease and line a 7" cake tin with greaseproof paper. Spoon the rice mixture into the cake tin and bake for 60 minutes. Remove from the oven and let it cool for 10 minutes before chilling in the fridge overnight.

Chocolate, Almond and Toffee Cake

Ingredients

For the cake

200 g / 7 oz / 1 ⅓ cups self-raising flour, sifted

225 g / 8 oz / 1 cup margarine, softened

225 g / 8 oz / 1 cup caster (superfine) sugar

55 g / 2 oz / ⅓ cup cocoa powder, sifted

4 large eggs

2 tbsp whole milk

1 tbsp cornflour, sifted

1 tsp vanilla extract

a pinch of salt

For the filling and icing

150 ml / 5 fl. oz / ⅔ cup dulce de leche

250 ml / 9 fl. oz / 1 cup double cream

240 g / 8 ½ oz / 1 ½ cups dark chocolate

55 g / 2 oz / ¼ cup caster (superfine) sugar

SERVES 8 | PREP TIME 15 minutes | COOKING TIME 25 minutes

Preheat the oven to 170°C (150° fan) / 325F / gas 3. Grease and line 2 x 7" tins. Combine all the ingredients for the cake in a bowl and beat for 2 minutes until smooth. Divide the batter evenly between the two cake tins.

Bake for 25 minutes then remove and cool. Place the sugar and cream in a saucepan and heat to boiling point. Place the chocolate in a bowl and pour over the cream mixture, stirring until you have a smooth ganache. Let it cool for 5 minutes.

Place one cake on a plate and spread the dulce de leche across it. Sandwich the other cake on top.

Pour the ganache on top of the cake and let it run all over it, down the sides, until it has covered the cake completely.

Let the ganache set as you prepare the garnish. Line a baking sheet with a sheet of greaseproof paper and prepare a sieve so that it is upturned on a flat surface. Place the sugar and cold water in a small saucepan and cook over a moderate heat, swirling occasionally, until the sugar has dissolved.

Cook the syrup until golden. Pour half on top of the paper and drizzle half on over the sieve in thin strands. Once set, remove and shape into a ball. Sit the ball on top of the cake and sprinkle the almonds. Chop the caramel on the baking sheet and sprinkle around the cake.

Breton Cake

Ingredients

225 g / 8 oz / 1 ½ cups plain (all-purpose)
flour, sifted
a little extra plain (all-purpose) flour
225 g / 8 oz / 1 cup caster (superfine) sugar
225 g / 8 oz / 2 sticks unsalted butter,
softened
6 large egg yolks
350 g / 12 oz / 2 ⅓ cups prunes
1 lemon, juiced
110 ml / 4 fl. oz / ½ cup water

SERVES 8 | PREP TIME 10-15 minutes | COOKING TIME 40-45 minutes

Preheat the oven to 180°C (160° fan) / 350F / gas 4. Prepare and measure all of the ingredients. Grease and line an 8" cake tin with greaseproof paper.

Combine the prunes, lemon juice and water in a saucepan. Heat over a medium heat, until simmering. Strain to get rid of the liquid, then pulse in a food processor until smooth. Spoon into a bowl, cover and chill.

Beat together the butter, sugar and egg yolks in a large mixing bowl until smooth.

Place the flour in a mound on a work surface and make a large well in its centre.

Add the egg and butter mixture to it and start working the flour into it to form a soft dough. Knead until you have an even, sticky dough.

Scoop half of the dough into the tin using floured hands. Spread the prune mix on top, then place the remaining dough on top. Bake for 30 minutes until golden. Remove and cool in the tin before turning out and serving.

Poppy Seed Cake

Ingredients

110 g / 4 oz / ⅔ cup self-raising flour, sifted

110 g / 4 oz / ½ cup caster (superfine) sugar

110 g / 4 oz / ½ cup margarine

30 g / 1 oz / ⅕ cup poppy seeds

2 large eggs

1 tsp orange flower water

a pinch of salt

SERVES 8 | PREP TIME 10 minutes | COOKING TIME 30-35 minutes

Preheat the oven to 170°C (150°C fan) /325F / gas 3. Measure and prepare all of the ingredients. .

Grease and line a 7" springform cake tin with greaseproof paper.

3

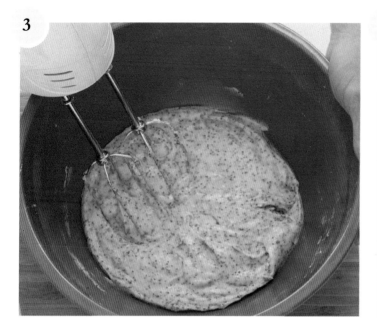

Combine all the ingredients for the cake in a large bowl and beat with an electric mixer for 2 minutes until smooth.

4

Spoon into the tin and drop a few times from a short height to help evenly distribute the batter in the tin. Bake for 25-35 minutes until golden and risen and a cake tester comes out clean from the centre.

5

Remove from the oven when ready and let the cake cool in the tin for 15 minutes.

6

Turn out onto a wire rack to finish cooling. Cut into slices when cool and serve on plates.

Pear Upside-down Cake

Ingredients

8 canned pear halves, drained

30 g / 1 oz / ¼ stick unsalted butter

30 g / 1 oz / 2 tbsp soft light brown sugar

For the batter

75 g / 3 oz / ¾ stick unsalted butter, softened

75 g / 3 oz / ⅓ cup sour cream

175 g / 6 oz / ¾ cup caster (superfine) sugar

150 g / 5 oz / 1 cup self-raising flour

1 tsp cornflour

3 medium eggs / 1 tsp vanilla extract

For the toffee sauce

110 g / 4 oz / ⅔ cup light brown soft sugar

110 g / 4 oz / 1 stick butter

75 ml / 3 fl. oz / ⅓ cup double cream

SERVES 8 | PREP TIME 15 minutes | COOKING TIME 50-60 minutes

Preheat the oven to 170°C (150°C fan) /325F / gas 3. Prepare and measure all of the ingredients. Melt 30 g of unsalted butter and 30 g soft light brown sugar together in a large saucepan set over a medium heat.

Add the pear halves and stir well. Grease and line the base of an 8" tin with greaseproof paper. Arrange the pears with their tops facing towards the centre of the tin. Pour over any remaining of the melted butter and sugar from the saucepan.

128

3

In a large bowl, combine the unsalted butter, sour cream, sugar, flour, eggs and vanilla extract. Beat until smooth using an electric hand-held whisk; usually 1-2 minutes.

4

Spoon into the tin and bake for 35-40 minutes until a cake tester comes out clean from the centre of the cake. Remove from the oven and allow to cool in the tin as you prepare the toffee sauce.

5

Melt the butter and sugar together over a low heat in a saucepan until the sugar has dissolved, stirring frequently. Add the cream, stirring well, then bring to a simmer.

6

Remove from the heat and set to one side to cool and thicken. Turn the cake out from the tin and arrange on a serving plate upside-down, so that the pears are facing upwards. Pour the toffee sauce into a serving jug and serve alongside the cake.

Sponge Cake

Ingredients

For the sponge cake

225 g / 8 oz / 1 ½ cups self-raising flour, sifted

225 g / 8 oz / 2 sticks unsalted butter, softened

225 g / 8 oz / 1 cup caster (superfine) sugar

4 large eggs

1 tsp lemon extract

1 tsp vanilla essence

a pinch of salt

110 g / 4 oz / ⅔ cup blueberries

For the lemon cream

225 g / 8 oz / 2 sticks unsalted butter, softened

250 g / 9 oz / 2 cups icing (confectioner's) sugar, sifted

2 lemons, juiced

To garnish

2 tbsp icing (confectioner's) sugar

SERVES 8 | PREP TIME 10-15 minutes | COOKING TIME 40-45 minutes

1

Preheat the oven to 170°C (150° fan) / 325F / gas 3. Grease and line two 8" cake tins with greaseproof paper. Prepare and measure all of the ingredients.

2

Combine all the ingredients for the sponge cake, apart from the blueberries, in a large mixing bowl.

Beat for 2 minutes until smooth, scraping down the sides from time to time.

Fold through the blueberries.

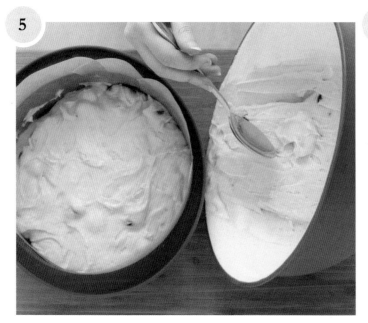

Divide the batter evenly between the tins. Bake for 25 minutes until golden. Remove from the oven and cool, whilst preparing the lemon cream.

Beat together the butter, icing sugar and lemon juice until smooth and fluffy. Spoon into a piping bag. Place one of the sponge cakes on a plate and pipe the cream on top. Sandwich the other sponge on top and dust with icing sugar.

Lemon Cake

Ingredients

For the cake batter

300 g / 10 ½ oz / 2 cups self-raising flour, sifted

225 g / 8 oz / 1 cup caster (superfine) sugar

4 medium eggs, beaten

150 ml / 5 fl. oz / ⅔ cup lemon juice

175 g / 6 oz / 1 ⅔ cup butter, softened

2 lemons, zested

55 ml / 2 fl. oz / ¼ cup whole milk

a pinch of salt

For the syrup

250 g / 9 oz / 2 cups icing (confectioner's) sugar

110 ml / 4 fl. oz / ½ cup lemon juice

For the icing and garnish

125 g / 4 ½ oz / 1 cup icing (confectioner's) sugar

75 ml / 3 fl. oz / ⅓ cup boiling water

½ lemon, thinly sliced

SERVES 8 | PREP TIME 15 minutes | COOKING TIME 60 minutes

Preheat the oven to 170°C (150° fan) / 325F / gas 3. Grease and line a loaf tin with greaseproof paper. Prepare and measure all of the ingredients.

Combine all the ingredients for the batter in a bowl and beat using an electric mixer until smooth; 1-2 minutes. Add a little milk and beat again briefly.

3

Spoon into the tin and bake for 1 hour. Remove from the oven when ready and leave to cool on a wire rack in the tin.

4

Whisk together the icing sugar and lemon juice in a saucepan until smooth. Heat over a low heat until the syrup starts to turn clear. Remove from the heat and leave to cool and thicken a little.

5

Pierce the lemon cake with a skewer all over and pour the syrup all over letting it sink in.

6

Whisk together the icing sugar and some boiling water in a mixing bowl, until you have a runny icing. Remove the lemon cake from the loaf tin and place on a presentation board.

7

Pour the icing on top and let it drip down the sides of the cake. Garnish the top with slices of lemon, arranging in a fan pattern on top before serving.

Sticky Toffee Pudding

Ingredients

200 g / 7 oz / 1 ⅓ cups fresh dates, pitted, chopped

225 g / 8 oz / 1 ½ cup self-raising flour

165 g / 5 ½ oz / ⅔ cup caster (superfine) sugar

300 g / 10 ½ oz / 1 ⅔ cups brown sugar

125 g / 4 ½ oz / 1 stick butter, diced

60 g / 2 ½ oz / ½ stick butter, softened

2 eggs

300 ml / 10 ½ fl. oz / 1 ¼ cup of crème fraîche

250 ml / 9 fl. oz / 1 cup of water

1 tsp bicarbonate of (baking) soda

1 tsp vanilla essence

butter, for greasing

SERVES 6 | PREP TIME 15 minutes | COOKING TIME 50 minutes

1

Preheat the oven to 180°C (160° fan) / 350F / gas 4. Brush a deep square cake pan with the melted butter to grease and line the base of the pan with non-stick baking paper.

2

Combine the water and dates in a small saucepan over medium heat and bring to the boil. Remove from the heat and stir in the bicarbonate of soda. Set aside to cool.

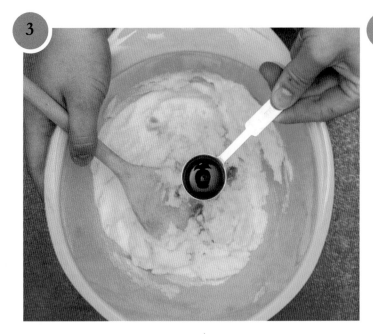

Beat the butter, sugar and vanilla essence in a large mixing bowl until creamy.

Add the eggs one at a time, beating well after each addition.

Fold in the sifted flour with a large metal spoon.

6

Fold the date mixture into the cake batter until combined.

7

Pour the mixture into the cake pan and bake for 45 minutes. Let it cool and unmold.

8

Combine the cream and brown sugar in a saucepan over medium heat, stirring until the sugar dissolves. Remove from the heat and stir in the butter until smooth. Serve with the warm butterscotch sauce accompanied by thick cream, if desired.

Frambosier

Ingredients

For the sponge cake

110 g / 4 oz / ⅔ cup self-raising flour, sifted

110 g / 4 oz / ½ cup caster (superfine) sugar

110 g / 4 oz / ½ cup margarine, softened

2 large eggs

1 tsp vanilla extract

a pinch of salt

For the filling and garnish

225 ml / 8 fl. oz / 1 cup double cream

1 tbsp icing (confectioner's) sugar

1 tbsp Framboise

1 tbsp caster (superfine) sugar

300 g / 10 ½ oz / 2 cups raspberries

30 g / 1 oz / 2 tbsp freeze-dried raspberries

SERVES 8 | PREP TIME 10-15 minutes | COOKING TIME 35-40 minutes

Preheat the oven to 180°C (160°C fan) / 350F / gas 4. Grease and line two 7" cake tins with greaseproof paper.

Combine all the ingredients for the cake in a bowl and beat with an electric mixer for a couple of minutes until smooth, scraping down the sides from time to time.

Divide the batter between the 2 tins and bake for 15-20 minutes until risen.

Prepare the filling by whipping together the cream, icing sugar and Framboise in a large mixing bowl until soft peaks form.

Remove the cakes from the oven and let them cool for 10 minutes before turning out onto a wire rack to finish cooling.

Place one of the sponge cakes on a plate and spread the cream on top. Stud with the raspberries, then place the other cake on top and sandwich together. Combine the freeze-dried raspberries and caster sugar in a food processor and pulse. Sprinkle on top of the cake before serving.

Fudge Tart

Ingredients

160 g / 5 ½ oz / 1 sheet ready-made
shortcrust pastry

a little plain (all-purpose) flour, for dusting

1 small egg, beaten

200 g / 7 oz / 1 ⅓ cups dark chocolate,
chopped

110 g / 4 oz / ½ cup caster (superfine) sugar

75 g / 3 oz / ¾ stick butter, cubed

55 g / 2 oz / ⅓ cup plain (all-purpose) flour,
sifted

4 small eggs

4 chocolate fudge bars, chopped

SERVES 8 | PREP TIME 10-15 minutes | COOKING TIME 45 minutes

Preheat the oven to 190°C (170° fan) / 375F / gas 5. Prepare and measure all of the ingredients. Roll the pastry out to 0.5 cm thick on a lightly floured work surface. Use it to line an 7" fluted tart tin.

Prick the base and line with greaseproof paper and baking beans. Blind bake for 15 minutes.

Remove and discard the paper and beans. Brush the base with the beaten egg and return to the oven for 2 minutes.

Meanwhile, combine the chocolate, butter and the fudge bars in a large heatproof bowl. Set the bowl over a saucepan over gently simmering water and stir occasionally until melted and smooth.

Beat together the melted butter, chocolate and fudge mixture with the eggs in a large mixing bowl until smooth. Add the flour and fold through until incorporated.

Reduce the oven to 170°C. Pour the chocolate filling into the tart and bake for 10 minutes until just set and glossy on top. Remove and allow it to cool for 10 minutes before chilling for 2 hours.

Pound Cake

Ingredients

110 g / 4 oz / ½ cup caster (superfine) sugar

110 g / 4 oz / ⅔ cup self-raising flour, sifted

55 g / 2 oz / ½ stick unsalted butter, softened

55 g / 2 oz / ¼ cup sour cream

110 g / 4 oz / ½ cup Mascarpone

2 large eggs

1 tsp vanilla extract

a pinch of salt

SERVES 6 | PREP TIME 10 minutes | COOKING TIME 30-35 minutes

Measure and prepare all of the ingredients. Preheat the oven to 170°C (150°C fan) /325F / gas 3.

Grease a 7" kugelhopf pan with a little cooking spray.

3

Combine the butter, sour cream, sugar, flour, eggs, Mascarpone and vanilla extract in a large mixing bowl.

4

Beat for 1-2 minutes using an electric mixer until smooth.

5

Spoon into the pan and bake for 25-30 minutes. Remove and allow the cake to cool in its tin for 10 minutes.

6

Carefully turn the cake out onto a wire rack after 10 minutes to let it cool a bit further.

Cheese Soufflé

Ingredients

55 g / 2 oz / ½ stick butter, softened

30 g / 1 oz / 2 tbsp plain (all-purpose) flour

250 ml / 9 fl. oz / 1 cup whole milk

4 large eggs, separated

1 tsp Dijon mustard

30 g / 1 oz / ¼ cup Gruyere, grated

30 g / 1 oz / ¼ cup Emmental, grated

55 g / 2 oz / ½ cup Comté, grated

salt and pepper

2 tbsp picked flat-leaf parsley leaves

SERVES 4 | PREP TIME 15 minutes | COOKING TIME 25-30 minutes

Preheat the oven to 200°C (180° fan) / 400F / gas 6. Grate the cheese into a bowl and leave to one side.

Brush the insides of 4 ceramic ramekins with half of the butter and chill until needed.

3

Melt the rest of the butter in a saucepan over a medium heat.

4

Whisk in the flour until you have a smooth roux. Cook the roux for 1-2 minutes, whisking occasionally.

5

Whisk in the milk in a slow, steady stream until you have a thickened sauce, then whisk in the egg yolks, mustard and most of the grated cheese until smooth.

6

Simmer for 5 minutes, add the parsley and adjusting the seasoning, then remove it from the heat. Whisk the egg whites in a clean mixing bowl with a pinch of salt until soft peaks form.

7

Fold the egg whites in to the sauce and mix well.

8

Spoon into the ramekins and sprinkle the tops with the remaining cheeses. Bake for 15 minutes until golden and risen. Serve immediately.

Lemon Meringue Pie

Ingredients

160 g / 5 ½ oz / 1 sheet shortcrust pastr
plain (all-purpose) flour, for dusting
1 small egg, beaten

For the filling

75 g / 3 oz / ⅓ cup caster (superfine) sugar
110 ml / 4 fl. oz / ½ cup lemon juice
55 g / 2 oz / ½ stick butter, cubed
1 tbsp cornflour
2 medium egg yolks
1 medium egg

For the meringue

2 small egg whites
110 g / 4 oz / ½ cup caster (superfine) sugar
1 tsp cornflour

SERVES 8 | PREP TIME 10-15 minutes | COOKING TIME 50-55 minutes

1

2

Prepare and measure out all of the ingredients. Preheat the oven to 190°C (170°C fan) / 375F / gas 5. Roll the pastry out to 0.5 cm thickness on a lightly floured work surface.

Line an 8" fluted tart tin with the pastry, pressing it into the base and sides well. Prick the base with a fork and trim the excess pastry from the edges.

3

Line with greaseproof paper and fill with baking beans, and then chill. Meanwhile, prepare the filling by combining the lemon juice, cornflour and sugar in a small saucepan.

4

Add 110 ml / 4 fl. oz / ½ cup of water and simmer, whisking continuously until the sauce thickens. Remove from the heat and beat in the butter until smooth and glossy. Whisk together the egg yolks and whole egg in a mixing bowl, then add to the lemon filling and return to the heat.

148

5

Continue to whisk until the mixture thickens. Remove from the heat and set to one side. Blind bake the pastry for 12 minutes. Remove from the oven and discard the paper and baking beans. Bake for 3 more minutes to brown the base. Remove from the oven and brush the base with the beaten egg to create a seal.

6

Leave to cool on a wire rack. Whisk the egg whites to soft peaks in a large bowl. Add half of the caster sugar, a bit at a time, beating well. Whisk in the cornflour, then the remaining sugar a bit at a time, whisking well until you have a thick, glossy meringue.

7

Spoon into a piping bag fitted with a 3 cm straight-sided nozzle. Reheat the lemon filling and spoon evenly between the pastry case.

8

Pipe blobs of the meringue all over the surface of the filling. Use the tip of a sharp knife to create spiky tails. Bake in the oven for 12-15 minutes until the meringue is golden at the tips. Remove and leave to sit for a few minutes before turning out and serving.

Apple Pie

Ingredients

160 g / 5 ½ oz / 1 sheet shortcrust pastry
a little plain (all-purpose) flour, for dusting
1 kg / 2 lb 4 oz / 4 ½ cups apples, peeled,
cored and sliced
30 g / 1 oz / ¼ stick unsalted butter
30 g / 1 oz / ¼ cup ground almonds
110 g / 4 oz / ⅔ cup soft light brown sugar
1 lemon, juiced
1 small egg, beaten

SERVES 6-8 | PREP TIME 15-20 minutes | COOKING TIME 35-40 minutes

1

Preheat the oven to 180°C (160°C fan) / 350F / gas 4. Melt the butter in a saucepan over a medium heat. Combine the apple, lemon juice and sugar in a large mixing bowl and toss until evenly coated.

2

Add to the melted butter and sauté for 3-4 minutes, tossing occasionally. Meanwhile, roll the pastry out into a 10" round on a lightly floured work surface.

3

Transfer to a large, round baking tray and sprinkle the ground almonds on the centre section.

4

Top with the slices of apple, overlapping them in the centre so that you leave the outer 3-4" of the pastry untouched.

5

Fold that pastry over and on top, back towards the centre so that it covers the apples; leaving an uncovered circle in the middle. Brush the pastry with beaten egg and bake for 25-30 minutes until the pastry is golden brown.

6

Remove and allow to cool for a few minutes on a wire rack before transferring to a serving plate.

Orange Cake

Ingredients

For the cake

200 g / 7 oz / 1 ⅓ cups self-raising flour, sifted

175 g / 6 oz / 1 ½ sticks unsalted butter, softened

175 g / 6 oz / ¾ cup golden caster (superfine) sugar

110g / 4 oz / ½ cup Greek yoghurt

3 large eggs

1 orange, juiced and zested

½ tsp orange flower water

30 g / 1 oz / 2 tbsp 'no peel' marmalade

For the orange syrup

200 g / 7 oz / 1 ½ cups icing (confectioner's) sugar

2 oranges, juiced

SERVES 8 | PREP TIME 15-20 minutes | COOKING TIME 70 minutes

Measure and prepare all of the ingredients. Preheat the oven to 180°C (160°C fan) / 350F / gas 4. Grease and line a 7" springform cake tin with greaseproof paper.

In a large bowl, beat together all the ingredients for the cake using an electric mixer until the batter just comes together.

3

Spoon into the tin and bake for 50-60 minutes. Remove from the oven and allow the cake to cool in the tin.

4

Meanwhile, combine the icing sugar and orange juice in a saucepan. Heat over a gentle heat until the sugar has dissolved and you have a syrup. Simmer the syrup for 2-3 minutes.

5

Remove from the heat and allow it to cool. Turn the cake out from the tin and puncture all over, using a skewer. Pour the syrup all over, allowing it to sink in and set on top of the cake before serving.

Marble Cake

Ingredients

For the chocolate cake batter

75 g / 3 oz / ½ cup plain flour, sifted

30 g / 1 oz / 2 tbsp cornflour, sifted

55 g / 2 oz / ¼ cup cocoa powder, sifted

110 g / 4 oz / ½ cup caster (superfine) sugar

110 g / 4 oz / ½ cup margarine, softened

2 large eggs

1 tbsp sour cream

For the vanilla cake batter

110 g / 4 oz / ⅔ cup self-raising flour, sifted

110 g / 4 oz / 1 stick unsalted butter, softened

110 g / 4 oz / ½ cup golden caster (superfine) sugar

2 large eggs

1 tbsp vanilla extract

a pinch of salt

To garnish

55 g / 2 oz / ⅓ cup dark chocolate, chopped

SERVES 8 | PREP TIME 10-15 minutes | COOKING TIME 70 minutes

Prepare and measure all of the ingredients. Preheat the oven to 170°C (150° fan) / 325C / gas 3. Grease and line the base and sides a 2 lb loaf tin with greaseproof paper.

Prepare the vanilla cake batter by combining all the ingredients for it in a large mixing bowl. Stir a few times with a wooden spoon before beating with an electric whisk for 2 minutes until smooth and even.

Set the batter to one side as you prepare the chocolate batter. Combine the flour, cornflour, cocoa, sugar, margarine and eggs in a bowl. Stir a few times with a wooden spoon before beating with an electric whisk for 2 minutes. Add the sour cream and beat again briefly.

Spoon half of the vanilla cake batter into the base of the prepared loaf tin. Top with all of the chocolate cake batter, then pour the remaining vanilla cake batter down one side of the tin on top of the chocolate cake batter.

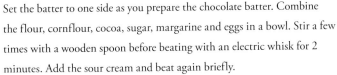

Use a cake tester to briefly swirl the top batters together. Bake for 50-60 minutes. Remove from the oven and let the cake cool in the tin set on top of a wire rack.

Once cool, turn the loaf out of the tin. Melt the chocolate in a microwave safe bowl, heating in 10 second bursts on full power, until melted and runny. Arrange the cake on a serving plate and pour the melted chocolate on top.

Chocolate Cake

Ingredients

For the sponge

225 g / 8 oz / 1 ½ cups self-raising flour, sifted

225 g / 8 oz / 1 cup margarine, softened

225 g / 8 oz / 1 cup caster (superfine) sugar

55 g / 2 oz / ⅓ cup cocoa powder

4 large eggs

55 ml / 2 fl. oz / ¼ cup whole milk

a pinch of salt

For the icing

350 g / 12 oz / 3 sticks unsalted butter

250 g / 9 oz / 2 cups icing (confectioner's) sugar, sifted

200 g / 7 oz / 1 ¼ cups good-quality dark chocolate, chopped

1 tsp vanilla essence

SERVES 8 | PREP TIME 10-15 minutes | COOKING TIME 45 minutes

Preheat the oven to 170°C (150° fan) / 325F / gas 3. Grease and line three 7" cake tins with greaseproof paper. Prepare and measure all of the ingredients.

Combine all the ingredients for the sponge in a bowl and beat together for 2-3 minutes until smooth.

Divide the batter evenly between the 3 tins and bake for 20 minutes until risen. Remove from the oven and let the sponges cool in their tins for 10 minutes.

Turn out onto wire racks to finish cooling; peel away any paper that is stuck to their bases.

Melt the icing chocolate in a heatproof bowl set over a saucepan of simmering water. Stir occasionally until melted, then remove from the heat and let it cool for 10 minutes.

Beat the ingredients for the icing in a bowl until fluffy. Add the chocolate and stir until smooth. Place one sponge on a plate and spread a third of the icing on top. Sandwich the second sponge on top and spread the top with half of the remaining icing. Sit the final sponge on top and spread the remaining icing on its top.

Chocolate Log Cake

Ingredients

For the sponge cake

110 g / 4 oz / ⅔ cup self-raising flour

110 g / 4 oz / 1 stick butter, softened

110 g / 4 oz / ½ cup golden caster (superfine) sugar

2 large eggs

2 tbsp whole milk

a pinch of salt

For the filling

300 ml / 10 ½ fl. oz / 1 ⅓ cups double cream

200 g / 7 oz / 1 ¼ cups milk chocolate

55 g / 2 oz / ½ stick unsalted butter, softened

For the icing

225 g / 8 oz / 1 ⅓ cups dark chocolate

225 ml / 8 fl. oz / 1 cup double cream

30 g / 1 oz / 2 tbsp soft brown sugar

1 tbsp corn syrup

1 tbsp glucose syrup

For decoration

55 g / 2 oz / ⅓ cup dark chocolate

1 tsp cocoa powder, for dusting

large handful of redcurrants

SERVES 8 | PREP TIME 15 minutes | COOKING TIME 60 minutes

Preheat the oven to 180°C (160° fan) / 350F / gas 4. Grease and line a 10" x 15" roll pan with greaseproof paper. Prepare and measure all of the ingredients.

Place the butter, sugar, salt and eggs in a bowl and sift the flour on top. Mix until smooth. Beat in the milk then spoon onto the roll pan.

3

Smooth until even then bake for 14 minutes until springy to the touch. Remove from the oven and allow to cool on a wire rack leaving the greaseproof paper attached to the base.

4

Heat the cream in a saucepan until it starts to boil. Place the chocolate in a heatproof bowl and pour the hot cream on top. Leave for 30 seconds then stir until smooth. Add the butter and stir. Leave to cool.

5

Melt 55 g of dark chocolate in a bain-marie set over a saucepan of simmering water. Stir until the chocolate is smooth then remove from the heat. Pour onto the back of a metal baking dish.

6

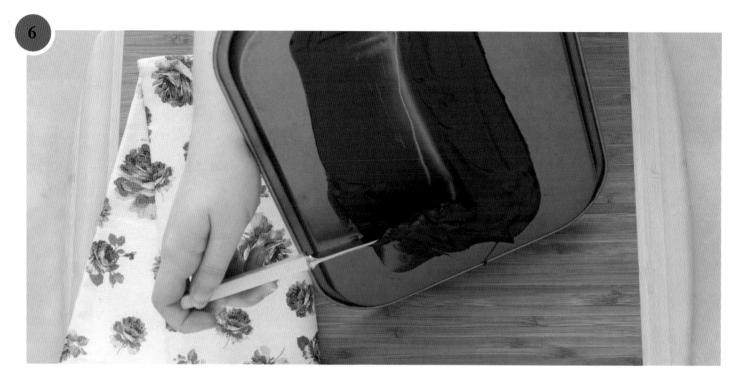

Spread the chocolate into a thin layer then leave to set. Push a spatula under the chocolate so that it curls then leave to one side. Spread the cake with the filling. Using the paper underneath as a guide, roll into a log shape.

7

Combine the cream, sugar and syrup in a saucepan. Bring to the boil then remove from the heat. Add the chocolate and melt for 1 minute. Stir until smooth. Let it cool before spreading all over the log. Let it cool then garnish with redcurrants and cocoa powder. Sit the curl on top.

Blueberry Pies

Ingredients

320 g / 11 oz / 2 sheets readymade shortcrust
pastry

a little plain (all-purpose) flour, for dusting

500 g / 1 lb 2 oz / 3 ⅓ cups blueberries

110 g / 4 oz / ½ cup caster (superfine) sugar

1 lemon, juiced

pinch of salt

To garnish

2 tbsp milk

1 tbsp caster (superfine) sugar

SERVES 4 | PREP TIME 10-15 minutes | COOKING TIME 55-60 minutes

Prepare and measure all of the ingredients. Roll half the pastry out on a lightly floured surface to roughly 1 cm thickness.

Cut 4 rounds of pastry that will line the base and sides of the 4 fluted tartlet or quiche moulds; roughly 12-14 cm in diameter.

Line the base and sides of the moulds with the pastry and trim any excess pastry; reserve and gather it up into a ball as you will need it later on.

Prick the base of the pastry and line with a sheet of greaseproof paper. Fill with baking beans and chill for 15 minutes.

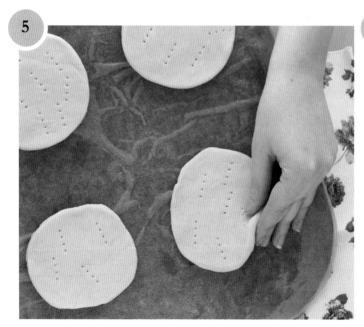

Preheat the oven to 180°C (160° fan) / 350F / gas 4. Roll the other half of pastry out on a floured surface, 1 cm thick and cut rounds 10 cm in diameter; these will be the lids for the pies. Prick the lids with a fork, then transfer to a tray lined with greaseproof paper. Chill until needed.

Prepare the filling by combining the blueberries, sugar, salt and lemon juice in a saucepan. Heat over a medium heat, stirring occasionally until you have a soft blueberry compote.

7

Let the compote cool to one side. Roll out the reserved excess pastry to 0.5 cm thickness on a lightly floured work surface. Use a sharp knife to cut into 10 cm x 1 cm x 0.5 cm strips. Spoon the blueberry compote into the pastry, then wet the rims of the pastry.

8

Sit the lids on top and seal well around the edges. Whisk together the milk and sugar in a small mixing bowl until dissolved. Brush the tops of the pies with some of the milk glaze.

9

Decorate the tops of the pies with the strips of reserved pastry. Place the pies on a tray and bake for 35-40 minutes until the pastry is golden. Remove from the oven and brush with the milk glaze. Let the pies cool in the moulds for 5-10 minutes before turning out and serving.

Orange and Marmalade Kumquat

Ingredients

160 g / 5 ½ oz / 1 sheet shortcrust pastry

a little plain flour, for dusting

450 g / 1 lb / 2 cups orange marmalade (jelly)

450 g / 1 lb / 3 cups kumquats, roughly chopped

2 oranges, juiced

1 small egg, beaten

To garnish

1 physallis

SERVES 8 | PREP TIME 10-15 minutes | COOKING TIME 70 minutes

1. Preheat the oven to 180°C (160° fan) / 350F / gas 4. Roll the pastry out on a floured surface to 0.5 cm thick. Line a pie tin with the pastry, pressing it into the edges and base. Trim the excess pastry and gather into a ball. Prick the base with a fork, then line with greaseproof paper and baking beans.

2. Chill for 15 minutes as you prepare the filling. Combine the kumquats, marmalade and orange juice in a large saucepan. Heat over a medium heat, stirring occasionally until the kumquats are soft.

Remove the saucepan from the heat and blend using a stick blender until you have a smooth, jam-like mixture.

Let the filling cool for 10-15 minutes.Remove the pastry from the fridge and discard the greaseproof paper and the baking beans. Fill with the cooled kumquat mixture so that it comes to the rim of the pie tin.

Roll the excess pastry out to 0.5 cm thick. Slice it into long strips, 1-2 cm wide. Layer them across the pie in a lattice pattern and brush with the beaten egg. Bake for 40 minutes. Garnish with physallis and serve.

Fig Cake

Ingredients

110 g / 4 oz / ½ cup caster (superfine) sugar

110 g / 4 oz / 1 stick unsalted butter, softened

200 g / 7 oz / 1 ⅓ cups plain (all-purpose) flour

125 ml / 4 ½ fl. oz / ½ cup water

125 g / 4 oz / ⅔ cup dried figs, roughly chopped

4 large fresh figs, roughly chopped

1 tsp baking powder

½ tsp ground mixed spice

a pinch of salt

SERVES 8 | PREP TIME 15 minutes | COOKING TIME 40 minutes

Preheat the oven to 180°C (160° fan) / 350F / gas 4. Prepare and measure all of the ingredients.

Combine the water, sugar, butter, fresh and dried figs in a large saucepan. Heat over a medium heat until the butter has melted and the sugar has dissolved.

Remove from the heat, then add the flour, baking powder and spice after a few minutes. Stir well to combine thoroughly.

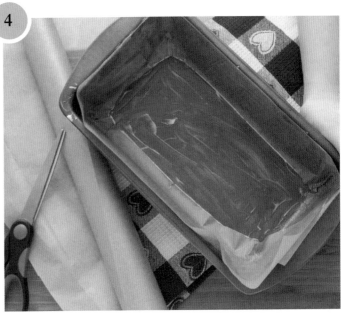

Grease and line the base and sides of a loaf tin.

Pour into the tin and bake for 40 minutes until a skewer comes out clean when inserted into the centre of the cake. Remove and allow to cool in the tin.

Once cool, turn the cake out carefully and peel away any greaseproof paper that has stuck to the cake. Slice and serve.

Plum Cake

Ingredients

800 g / 1 lbs 12 oz / 4 cups Mirabelle plums, de-stoned

240 ml / 8 fl. oz / 1 cup plain yoghurt

110 g / 4 oz / ½ cup caster (superfine) sugar

75 ml / 3 fl. oz / ⅓ cup vegetable oil

450 g / 1 lb / 3 cups plain (all-purpose) flour, sifted

2 medium eggs

1 ½ tsp baking powder

½ tsp bicarbonate (baking) of soda

a pinch of salt

SERVES 8 | PREP TIME 15-20 minutes | COOKING TIME 45-55 minutes

Prepare and measure all of the ingredients. Preheat the oven to 180°C (160° fan) / 350F / gas 4.

Grease and line an 8" springform tin with greaseproof paper.

3

In a mixing bowl, whisk together the yoghurt, sugar, eggs and oil. In another mixing bowl, combine the flour, baking powder, bicarbonate of soda and salt. Combine the wet and dry ingredients together folding together until smooth.

4

Spoon the batter into the cake tin and drop the plums on top so that they sink into the batter.

5

Bake for 35-45 minutes until the cake is golden on top and a cake tester comes out clean from the centre. Remove from the oven and leave to cool in the tin for 10 minutes.

6

Turn out and move to a wire rack to finish cooling. Serve warm or cold.

Cherry Pies

Ingredients

320 g / 11 oz / 2 sheets shortcrust pastry

a little plain (all-purpose) flour, for dusting

450 g / 1 lb / 2 cups canned griotte cherries, drained

30 ml / 1 fl. oz / 2 tbsp whole milk

1 tbsp caster (superfine) sugar

SERVES 4 | PREP TIME 20-25 minutes | COOKING TIME 45-50 minutes

Prepare and measure all of the ingredients. Roll half the pastry out on a lightly floured surface to roughly 1 cm thickness.

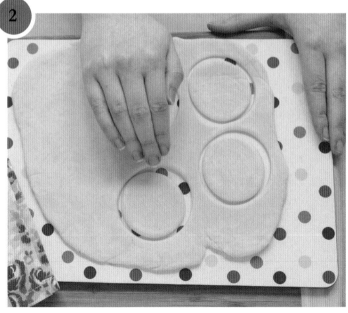

Cut 4 rounds of pastry that will line the base and sides of the moulds of a cupcake tin; roughly 10 cm in diameter.

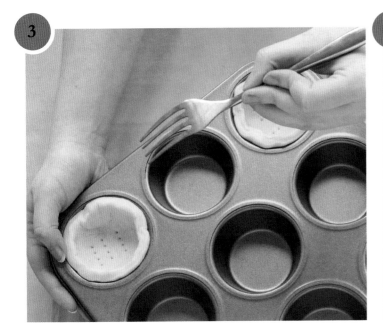

Line 4 moulds of a cupcake tin with the pastry and trim any excess pastry. Prick the base of the pastry and chill for 15 minutes. Preheat the oven to 180°C (160° fan) / 350F / gas 4.

Roll the other half of pastry out to roughly 1 cm in thickness and cut rounds 5 cm in diameter; these will be the lids for the pies. Prick the pastry lids a few times with a fork. Remove the chilled pastry from the fridge and spoon the drained cherries into them.

Carefully place the pastry lids on top and crimp the edges together to secure. Bake for 25-30 minutes. Meanwhile, whisk together the milk and sugar to make a glaze. Remove the pies from the oven and brush the tops with the glaze. Return to the oven for a few minutes. Remove from the oven and leave to cool in the mould for 5 minutes before turning out and serving.

Brownie Yoghurts

Ingredients

300 ml / 10 ½ fl. oz / 1 ⅓ cups natural
yoghurt, stirred

350 g / 12 oz / 2 cups good-quality dark
chocolate, chopped

225 g / 8 oz / 2 sticks unsalted butter

250 g / 9 oz/ 1 ⅓ cups light soft brown sugar

110 g / 4 oz / ⅔ cup plain (all-purpose) flour

3 large eggs

1 tsp baking powder

a pinch of salt

SERVES 4 | PREP TIME 15 minutes | COOKING TIME 40 minutes

Preheat the oven to 170°C (150° fan) / 325F / gas 3. Grease and line the base of a 5" square baking tray. Prepare and measure all of the ingredients.

Melt the chocolate and butter together in a saucepan over a medium-low heat, stirring occasionally until they are smooth. Remove from the heat and allow to cool a little.

In a large bowl, whisk the eggs until they are thick then add the sugar and continue to whisk until glossy. Beat in the melted chocolate mixture, then fold in the flour and baking powder until incorporated.

Pour into the tray and tap lightly a few times to release any trapped air bubbles. Bake for 40 minutes until the surface has set. Remove from the oven and cool on a wire rack for 45 minutes.

Once cool, turn out of the tin onto a chopping board. Cut the block of brownie in half and lightly break up one half with a fork, moving the broken-up brownie to a small bowl.

Cut the remaining half into even squares for presentation. Divide half of the broken-up brownie between the bases of 4 small serving glasses.

Top each with 2 tbsp of yoghurt. Spoon 1 tbsp of the broken-up brownie on top of the yoghurt, then top with 2 tbsp of yoghurt. Sprinkle crumbs from the broken-up brownie on top. Serve alongside the brownie squares.

Chocolate and Almond Moelleux

Ingredients

30 g / 1 oz / ¼ stick butter, melted

110 g / 4 oz / ⅔ cup good-quality dark chocolate, chopped

110 g / 4 oz / 1 stick unsalted butter, cubed

75 g / 3 oz / ½ cup plain (all-purpose) flour

30 g / 1 oz / 2 tbsp cocoa powder

30 g / 1 oz / ¼ cup ground almonds

2 medium eggs

2 medium egg yolks

To garnish

4 tbsp flaked (slivered) almonds, to garnish

SERVES 4 | PREP TIME 10-15 minutes | COOKING TIME 25-30 minutes

Preheat the oven to 190°C (170° fan) / 375F / gas 5. Measure and prepare all of the ingredients.

Brush four ovenproof ramekins with some of the melted butter, making sure to use upwards strokes with the pastry brush.

3

Chill the ramekins for 15 mins then brush with another layer of melted butter. Dust the insides with the cocoa powder, tapping lightly to get rid of any excess.

4

Chill until ready to fill with the batter. Prepare the batter by melting together the chocolate and cubed butter in a heatproof mixing bowl set over a pan of gently simmering water.

5

Once melted, remove from the heat and allow to cool for 10 minutes. Meanwhile, whisk together the eggs and egg yolks in a separate bowl. Sift the plain flour into the eggs and whisk until smooth, then fold in the ground almonds until combined.

6

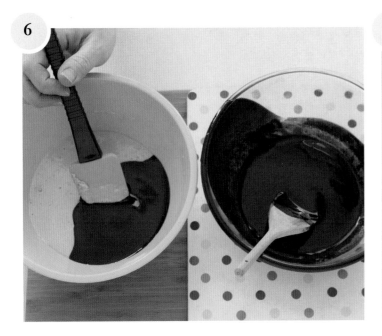

Pour the chocolate into the egg, flour and almond mixture in thirds, mixing well between each addition.

7

Divide the fondant batter evenly between the chilled moulds and arrange on a baking sheet. Bake in the oven for 10-12 minutes until the tops are set and the edges are starting to come away from the sides of the ramekins.

8

Remove from the oven and allow to sit for a few minutes. Garnish with the flaked almonds on top before serving.

Corn Cake

Ingredients

175 g / 6 oz / 1 1/6 cups self-raising flour, sifted

110 g / 4 oz / 1 stick unsalted butter, melted

55 ml / 2 fl. oz / 1/4 cup sunflower oil

225 g / 8 oz / 1 cup canned sweetcorn, drained

2 large eggs

1 tsp bicarbonate (baking) of soda

1 tsp baking powder

1 tsp salt

SERVES 8 | PREP TIME 10 minutes | COOKING TIME 45-55 minutes

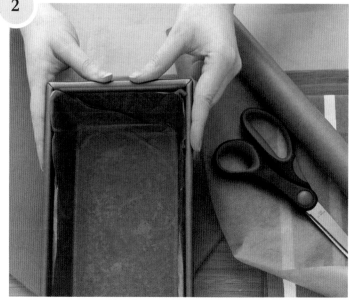

Measure and prepare all of the ingredients. Preheat the oven to 170°C (150°C fan) /325F / gas 3.

Grease and line a 2 lb loaf tin with greaseproof paper.

3

Combine the flour, baking powder, bicarbonate of soda, salt and sweetcorn in a large mixing bowl.

4

Whisk together the eggs, melted butter and sunflower oil in a jug until smooth.

5

Add the wet ingredients to the dry ones and mix well until smooth.

6

Spoon the batter into the tin and bake for 40-50 minutes. Remove from the oven and leave to cool for 15-20 minutes before turning out onto a wire rack to finish cooling.

Summer Fruits Tart

Ingredients

160 g / 5 ½ oz / 1 sheet readymade shortcrust pastry

plain (all-purpose) flour, for dusting

150 ml / 5 fl. oz / ⅔ cup whole milk

150 ml / 5 fl. oz / ⅔ cup double cream

110 g / 4 oz / ½ cup caster (superfine) sugar

30 g / 1 oz / 2 tbsp plain (all-purpose) flour

3 small egg yolks

2 small whole eggs

110 g / 4 oz / ⅔ cup raspberries

55 g / 2 oz / ⅓ cup blueberries

55 g / 2 oz / ⅓ cup blackberries

30 g / 1 oz / 2 tbsp redcurrants

To garnish

1 tbsp granulated sugar

1 tbsp icing (confectioner's) sugar

SERVES 4 | PREP TIME 20 minutes | COOKING TIME 30 minutes

Preheat the oven to 180°C (160° fan) / 350F / gas 4. Wash the berries and place in a colander. Dust a work surface with a little flour.

Roll the pastry out to 0.25 cm thick. Cut 4 rounds and use to line 4 heart-shaped moulds, pressing the pastry into the base and sides. Prick the all over with a fork and line with greaseproof paper.

Fill with baking beans and chill for 15 minutes. Combine the milk and cream in a saucepan and bring to a simmer. Once simmering, remove from the heat and set to one side.

In a bowl, whisk together the egg yolks and eggs until light and frothy. Add the sugar and whisk well, then sift in the flour and whisk until smooth. Gradually add the milk and cream to the egg mixture and whisk until smooth.

Remove the moulds from the fridge and arrange on a baking sheet. Blind bake for 15 minutes until they colour at the edges. Remove from the oven and discard the greaseproof paper and the baking beans. Fill the pastries with the mixture of the berries.

Pour the batter evenly on top. Bake for 15 minutes until the filling sets. Remove from the oven and cool on a wire rack. Dust with the icing and granulated sugars.

Yoghurt and Fruit Cake

Ingredients

150 ml / 5 fl. oz / ⅔ cup plain yoghurt

110 g / 4 oz / ½ cup caster (superfine) sugar

75 ml / 3 fl. oz / ⅓ cup vegetable oil

200 g / 7 oz / 1 ⅓ cups plain (all-purpose) flour, sifted

55 g / 2 oz / ½ cup ground almonds

110 g / 4 oz / ½ cup sultanas

30 g / 1 oz / 2 tbsp dried cranberries

110 g / 4 oz / ⅔ cup walnuts, chopped

2 medium eggs

1 ½ tsp baking powder

½ tsp bicarbonate (baking) soda

a pinch of salt

SERVES 8 | PREP TIME 10-15 minutes | COOKING TIME 45 minutes

Preheat the oven to 180°C (160° fan) / 350F / gas 4. Grease and line a loaf tin with greaseproof paper. Prepare and measure all of the ingredients.

In a bowl, whisk together the yoghurt, sugar, eggs and oil.

In another mixing bowl, combine the flour, baking powder, baking soda and salt.

Combine the wet and dry ingredients together, cutting and folding until you have a smooth batter.

Add the sultanas, cranberries, walnuts and ground almonds and continue to cut and fold until well incorporated.

Spoon into the tin and bake for 45 minutes. Remove from the oven and cool in the tin for 10 minutes before turning out onto a wire rack to finish cooling.

Strawberry Paris Brest

Ingredients

300 ml / 10 ½ fl. oz / 1 ⅓ cups water

150 g / 5 oz / 1 cup plain (all-purpose) flour, sifted

110 g / 4 oz / 1 stick unsalted butter, softened

4 medium eggs

2 tbsp caster (superfine) sugar

3-4 tbsp flaked (slivered) almonds

a pinch of salt

To garnish

450 g / 1 lb / 2 cups strawberries, hulled

300 ml / 10 ½ fl. oz / 1 ⅓ cups double cream

2 tbsp icing (confectioner's) sugar

½ tsp vanilla extract

SERVES 8 | PREP TIME 10-15 minutes | COOKING TIME 45-50 minutes

Preheat the oven to 200°C (180° fan) / 400F / gas 6. Prepare and measure all of the ingredients. Grease a couple of baking trays with a little sunflower oil.

Heat the water and butter in a saucepan over a medium heat until the butter melts. Add the flour, salt and sugar and beat until the mixture starts to leave the side of the pan. Beat in most of the eggs, until you have a smooth mixture.

3

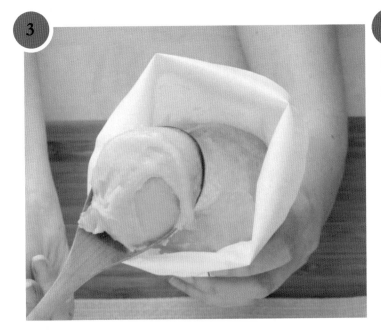

Keep any leftover beaten egg for glazing the pastry. Transfer the pastry into a piping bag fitted with a straight nozzle tip 4 cm in diameter.

4

Pipe a 20 cm (diameter) ring onto the baking tray and then pipe another ring of pastry inside the first ring making sure that it borders the inside of the other ring.

5

Pipe a ring of pastry on top of the two rings of pastry so that it sits between the join on top of them. Glaze the pastry ring with the remaining beaten egg and sprinkle the top with the flaked almonds. Bake for 20-25 minutes.

6

Remove from the oven when ready and let it cool on a wire rack. Whip together the cream with the vanilla extract in a large mixing bowl until it forms soft peaks. Spoon the whipped cream into a piping bag.

7

Remove the top of the pastry ring from the wider base using a sharp knife. Pipe whipped cream and place strawberries all over the base. Sit the remaining pastry ring on top of this, so that it rests on the strawberries. Dust with icing sugar before serving.

Sugar Bun

Ingredients

900 g / 2 lb / 6 cups strong plain white flour

4 tsp fast action dried yeast

½ tsp salt

55 g / 2 oz / ½ stick butter, cubed

150 ml / 5 fl. oz / ⅔ cup whole milk, warmed

450 ml / 16 fl. oz / 2 cups lukewarm water

To garnish

110 ml / 4 fl. oz / ½ cup whole milk

55 g / 2 oz / ⅓ cup sugar nibs

MAKES 4 | PREP TIME 10-15 minutes | COOKING TIME 70 minutes

Combine the flour, salt and dried yeast in a large mixing bowl.

Rub the butter into the flour mixture using your fingertips until you have a mixture resembling fine breadcrumbs.

Combine the warm milk and water in a jug and pour into the flour mixture, mixing well with a wooden spoon until you have a soft dough.

Turn out onto a lightly floured work surface and knead for 10-15 minutes until you have a smooth, elastic dough.

Place the dough in a large mixing bowl and cover with a damp tea towel. Leave to rise in a warm place. After 1 hour, remove from the bowl and knock it down using your hands. Divide into 4 oval buns and arrange on lightly greased baking trays.

Cover with pieces of oiled film, leaving them to prove in a warm place for a further hour until doubled in size again.

Preheat the oven to 220°C (200°C fan) / 425F / gas 7. Remove the film and bake for 20-25 minutes until golden and risen; they are ready when they sound hollow when tapped on their undersides.

Remove from the oven and brush with the milk.

For the garnish, sprinkle the sugar nibs on top so that they stick. Let the buns cool on a wire rack before serving.

Index

all spice
Raisin Cookies 12
almonds, blanched
Almond Cookies 22
Petit Fours 18
almond, extract
Chocolate Fudge Cake 110
Petit Fours 18
almonds, flaked (slivered)
Chocolate and Almond
Moelleux 175
Strawberry Paris Brest 184
almonds, ground
Almond Cookies 22
Amaretti 54
Apple Pie 150
Blackberry and Raspberry
Cakes 66
Chocolate and Almond
Moelleux 175
Chocolate Fudge Cake 110
Chocolate Pudding 107
King's Cakes 40
Petit Fours 18
Sweet Macaroons 50
Yoghurt and Fruit Cake 182
amaretto liqueur
Amaretti 54
apples, Bramley

Apple Pie 150
Apple Toffee Muffins 56
Stewed Apple Muffins 8

baking powder
Blueberry Muffins 6
Brownie Yoghurts 172
Cheese Loaf 98
Cheese Scones 100
Chocolate and Pecan Muffins 14
Chocolate and Walnut
Sponge 114
Chocolate Chip Cookies 26
Corn Cake 178
Fig Cake 166
Hazelnut Brownies 32
Herb Cakes 64
Lemon Muffins 10
Plum Cake 168
Scones 47
Stewed Apple Muffins 8
Yoghurt and Fruit Cake 182
basil, dried
Parmesan and Basil Rolls 94
basil, leaves
Parmesan and Basil Rolls 94
bicarbonate of soda
Almond Cookies 22

Apple Pie 150
Apple Toffee Muffins 56
Chocolate Chip Cookies 26
Chocolate Shortbread 62
Coconut Cookies 20
Corn Cake 178
Honey Scones 16
Plum Cake 168
Shortbread 30
Sticky Toffee Pudding 135
blackberries
Blackberry and Raspberry
Cakes 66
Summer Fruits Tart 180
blueberries (bilberries)
Bilberry Pie 112
Blueberry Muffins 6
Blueberry Pies 161
Sponge Cake 130
Summer Fruits Tart 180

carrots
Carrot and Cinnamon Cake 116
cheese, cheddar
Walnut and Cheese Loaf 76
cheese, Comte
Cheese Soufflé 144
cheese, cream
Lemon Muffins 10
Thyme Macaroons 52

cheese, Emmenthal
Cheese Soufflé 144
cheese, Gouda
Gouda Loaf 86
cheese Gruyere
Cheese Loaf 98
Cheese Soufflé 144
Cheese Sticks 80
Walnut and Cheese Loaf 76
cheese, Marscapone
Pound Cake 142
cheese, Parmesan
Cheese Loaf 98
Herb Cakes 64
Parmesan and Basil Rolls 94
cheese, Ricotta
Italian Rice Tart 120
Spinach Savoury Cake 78
Thyme Macaroons 52
cheese, Roquefort
Cheese Scones 100
Thyme Macaroons 52
cherries, canned
Cherry Pies 170
chocolate, chips
Chocolate Chip Cookies 26
Chocolate Cookies 28

chocolate, dark

Brownie Yoghurts 172

Chocolate, Almond and Toffee Cake 122

Chocolate and Almond Moelleux 175

Chocolate and Pecan Muffins 14

Chocolate and Walnut Sponge 114

Chocolate Cake 156

Chocolate Fudge Cake 110

Chocolate Log Cake 158

Chocolate Pudding 107

Fudge Tart 140

Hazelnut Brownies 32

Marble Cake 154

Mocha Cake 104

Pistachio Brownies 60

Sweet Macaroons 50

chocolate, milk

Chocolate Log Cake 158

cinnamon, ground

Carrot and Cinnamon Cake 116

Oatmeal Cookies 38

cloves, ground

Raisin Cookies 12

cocoa powder

Chocolate, Almond and Toffee Cake 122

Chocolate and Almond Moelleux 175

Chocolate and Walnut Sponge 114

Chocolate and Pecan Muffins 14

Chocolate Cake 156

Chocolate Cookies 28

Chocolate Log Cake 158

Chocolate Shortbread 62

Chocolate Pudding 107

Marble Cake 154

Mocha Cake 104

Pistachio Brownies 60

Sweet Macaroons 50

coconut, dessicated

Coconut Cookies 20

Pineapple Coconut Tart 118

coffee, granules

Mocha Cake 104

cream, double

Bilberry Pie 112

Chocolate, Almond and Toffee Cake 122

Chocolate Log Cake 158

Frambosier 138

Pear Upside-down Cake 128

Shortbread 30

Strawberry Paris Brest 184

Summer Fruits Tart 180

Sweet Macaroons 50

Viennese Whirls 58

Violet and Orange Soufflé 44

courgette

Courgette and Rosemary Foccacia 96

cream, sour

Marble Cake 154

Pear Upside-down Cake 128

Pound Cake 142

cream, of tartar

Honey Scones 16

crème fraiche

Sticky Toffee Pudding 135

cumin, seeds

Cheese Sticks 80

Gouda Loaf 86

dates

Sticky Toffee Pudding 135

dulce de leche

Chocolate, Almond and Toffee Cake 122

Apple Toffee Muffins 56

figs, dried

Fig Cake 166

figs, fresh

Fig Cake 166

flax seeds

Granary Bread 68

framboise

Frambosier 138

ginger, crystallized in syrup

Mini Ginger Cakes 35

ginger, root

Mini Ginger Cakes 35

ham, Parma

Olive Bread Sticks 90

hazelnuts

Hazelnut Brownies 32

Italian Rice Tart 120

honey

Gouda Loaf 86

Granary Bread 68

Honey Scones 16

Oatmeal Cookies 38

Poppy Seed Palmiers 24

Sweetcorn Bread 72

jam, apricot

King's Cakes 40

Pineapple Coconut Tart 118

jam, strawberry

Viennese Whirls 58

kumquats

Orange and Marmalade Kumquat 164

mint, fresh

Shortbread 30

mixed spice, ground

Fig Cake 166

mustard, Dijon

Cheese Soufflé 144

nutmeg

Carrot and Cinnamon Cake 116

parsley, fresh

Cheese Soufflé 144

Herb Cakes 64

pastry, puff

Cheese Sticks 80

King's Cakes 40

Poppy Seed Palmiers 24

pastry, shortcrust

Apple Pie 150

Bilberry Pie 112

Blueberry Pies 161

Cherry Pies 170

Fudge Tart 140

Lemon Meringue Pie 147

Orange and Marmalade Kumquat 164

Pineapple Coconut Tart 118

Summer Fruits Tart 180

pears

Pear Upside-down Cake 128

pecans

Chocolate and Pecan Muffins 14

Pistachio Brownies 60

peppercorns, pink

Thyme Macaroons 52

physallis

Orange and Marmalade Kumquat 164

pine nuts

Spinach Savoury Cake 78

pineapple, rings

Pineapple Coconut Tart 118

pistachios, chopped

Pistachio Brownies 60

plums, Mirabelle

Plum Cake 168

poppy seeds

Poppy Seed Cake 126

Poppy Seed Loaf 82

Poppy Seed Palmiers 24

prunes

Breton Cake 124

raisins

Raisin Cookies 12

Scones 47

raspberries

Blackberry and Raspberry Cakes 66

Frambosier 138

Shortbread 30

Summer Fruits Tart 180

redcurrants

Chocolate Log Cake 158

Summer Fruits Tart 180

rice, Arborio

Italian Rice Tart 120

rosemary

Rosemary Focaccia 88

Courgette and Rosemary Foccacia 96

rum

Chocolate Fudge Cake 110

Pineapple Coconut Tart 118

sesame seeds

Honey Scones 16

Sesame Seed Rolls 102

spinach, fresh

Spinach Savoury Cake 78

strawberries

Strawberry Paris Brest 184

sugar, nibs

Sugar Bun 187

sultanas

Yoghurt and Fruit Cake 182

sunflower seeds

Granary Bread 68

sweetcorn

Corn Cake 178

Sweetcorn Bread 72

syrup, corn

Chocolate Log Cake 158

syrup, glucose

Chocolate and Walnut Sponge 114

Chocolate Fudge Cake 110

Chocolate Log Cake 158

syrup, golden

Carrot and Cinnamon Cake 116

tarragon, fresh

Herb Cakes 64

thyme, dried

Thyme Macaroons 52

thyme, leaves

Thyme Macaroons 52

tomato, puree

Tomato Bread 70

tomatoes, sun-dried

Tomato Bread 70

walnuts

Chocolate and Walnut Sponge 114

Walnut and Cheese Loaf 76

Walnut Bread 92

Yoghurt and Fruit Cake 182

walnut oil

Walnut and Cheese Loaf 76

Walnut Bread 92

yoghurt, natural/plain

Blueberry Muffins 6

Brownie Yoghurts 172

Orange Cake 152

Plum Cake 168

Yoghurt and Fruit Cake 182